RABBI DAVID KIMHI'S

COMMENTARY

UPON THE

PROPHECIES OF ZECHARIAH.

TRANSLATED FROM THE HEBREW.

WITH NOTES, AND OBSERVATIONS ON THE PASSAGES
RELATING TO THE MESSIAH.

BY THE REV. A. M'CAUL, A.M.,
OF TRINITY COLLEGE, DUBLIN.

Wipf & Stock
PUBLISHERS
Eugene, Oregon

Wipf and Stock Publishers
199 W 8th Ave, Suite 3
Eugene, OR 97401

Commentary upon the Prophecies of Zechariah
By Kimhi, David
ISBN 13: 978-1-55635-329-11
ISBN 10: 1-55635-329-4
Publication date 4/4/2007
Previously published by James Duncan, 1837

TO

THE PEOPLE OF ISRAEL,

A NATION NOT MORE REMARKABLE

FOR

THE CALAMITIES WHICH THEY HAVE SURVIVED,

THAN FOR

A GENIUS AND LOVE OF LEARNING

WHICH THOSE CALAMITIES COULD NEVER SUBDUE,

This Specimen

OF

ONE OF THEIR COMMENTARIES

IS

AFFECTIONATELY INSCRIBED,

BY

THE TRANSLATOR

INTRODUCTION.

RABBI DAVID KIMCHI, commonly called by the Jews from the three initial letters רד״ק RaDaK, was probably born at Narbonne, where his father lived.* Reland † considers it doubtful, because, in his printed and manuscript works, he calls himself, "David, the son of Joseph, the son of Kimchi the Spaniard," whereas Narbonne is in France. But the vicinity to Spain, and the fact that his family was Spanish, and that he himself was altogether identified with the Spanish school of Hebrew learning, would fully warrant this title. ‡ But, however that be, it is certain that his life and labours present an interesting incident in the literary history of an eventful period.

* Jost (in his Geschichte der Israeliten, vol. vi. 104) says unhesitatingly, that he was born there, but the only authority which he gives is that of Wolfius, who does not speak so positively.

† Vitæ celeb. Rab. p. 81, 82, in his Analecta.

‡ Wolfius, in his account of Joseph Kimchi, the father, says, "Hispanus, Narbonæ, quæ tum temporis Hispanis parebat."—Bibliothec. Heb. part i. p. 562.

He flourished about the time of the third Crusade, A.D. 1190, and lived through the first quarter of the thirteenth century. Whilst the laity of Christendom were engaged in the attempt to recover the Holy City, and the divines in perfecting and systematising the Christian oral law, or Popish Rabbinism, Kimchi, and other distinguished rabbies of the day, were zealously and laboriously employed in the grammatical study of the Old Testament, and in the improvement of biblical interpretation. Their countrymen were accustomed then, as now, wherever the Talmud is much studied, to follow the Talmudic method of interpretation, and to pay but little attention either to context or grammar, of which, from the method of instruction pursued in Rabbinical schools, they do not so readily perceive the necessity or the value. It would, however, be a mistake to suppose that Kimchi or his cotemporaries had discovered the simple and rational method of exposition, or that the Jews, in the long interval between the dispersion and the Crusades, were either ignorant or destitute of the grammatical principle. They carried with them from their country Onkelos's Chaldee translation * of the Pentateuch, as a model of literal interpretation; and the labours of Jonathan, † about two centuries after the dispersion, testify that they knew how to profit by it. The Masora ‡ furnishes another instance of a diligent and accurate grammatical study of the text. "It is evident," says Gesenius, §

* Known by the name of Targum of Onkelos.

† Jonathan Ben Uzziel's Targum on the Prophets.

‡ See Buxtorf's Tiberias, or Masoretic Commentary.

§ Geschichte der Heb. Sprache. p. 75. On the following page he "that its authors were guided by fixed grammatical principles, which, though never collected into one whole, they had deduced for themselves, and according to which they conformed the text, and endeavoured to remove its irregularities and supposed errors. In doing so, they manifest a great accuracy of study."

The punctuation, whenever affixed, presupposes no scanty measure of grammatical study; and the system of the accents shows the most accurate and delicate perception of the relation and connexion of words and sentences; and these two together must have ever preserved amongst the reflecting Jews a correct taste for the true principles of interpretation. These works attest the continued existence of grammatical principles amongst the Jews themselves, but it is probable that from the Arabic grammarians they learned method and system;* and soon after the triumphs of Mahometanism, and the culture of Arabic, the series of professed Jewish grammarians commenced.† About the beginning of the tenth century, Saadiah Gaon distinguished himself as a grammarian, translator, and commentator, from whom the succeeding commentators often make useful citations. In the latter half of the eleventh century, R. Solomon, commonly called Rashi, furnished a commentary to the

states his opinion that this work was diligently carried on in the sixth century, and finished about the eighth or ninth.

* It may, however, be doubted whether the benefit was an unmixed good; and whether, if the Jews had worked out their own principles to a system, that system would not have been more purely Hebrew, and therefore more correct.

† Gesen. Geschichte, p. 94.

whole Bible, which, though full of Talmudisms, manifests diligence, acuteness, a thorough acquaintance with the language of Scripture, and a desire to rise above Talmudic interpretation. He was succeeded in the next century by Aben Ezra, who far surpassed him in power and freedom of judgment. And a little later came David Kimchi, who, diligently using the labours of his predecessors, and possessing no ordinary resources of his own, has, besides a grammar and lexicon, left a commentary on most of the books of Scripture, which, though written six hundred years ago, will bear a comparison with any that has appeared even in the nineteenth century. Valuable in itself, it has other points of attraction for the Christian student. It is the work of one to whom the Christian world has been much indebted; for his grammar and lexicon have, until very lately, contributed the main portion of all similar productions, and his commentary has been one of the sources from which commentators since the Reformation have drawn most valuable materials. What Gesenius says generally of the Jewish commentators is particularly true of Kimchi. "The judicious commentator will know how to use much in them that is indisputably true and good; and a facility in understanding these sources is indispensably necessary to every respectable interpreter." * To the reader of the English Bible, Kimchi is also of value, as he will find the translations generally confirmed, and see how very little that rabbi would have altered. Indeed, a comparison with the rabbies would show that our translators were deeply read in, and diligent in consulting the best Jewish autho-

* Gesen. Geschichte, p. 102.

rities, and would go far towards proving that we have great reason to be satisfied with, and thankful for, our English translation. To the student of divinity, Kimchi and his cotemporaries are of great importance, inasmuch as they may be regarded as the founders of a new school in Jewish theology. The violent persecutions of the Crusaders, the jealousy excited by the Christian attempt upon the Holy Land, and the influence of the doctrine of the Mahometans, amongst whom they lived, produced a sensible change in Jewish opinions and interpretations, which is plainly marked in Kimchi, and other writers of the day, and without a knowledge of which, the phænomena of modern Judaism connot be fully understood. Rashi, Aben Ezra, and Kimchi endeavoured to get rid of the Christian interpretations, and Maimonides to root out the Christian doctrines which had descended from the ancient Jewish Church. The writings of the commentators passed without notice, but Maimonides' attack on Jewish doctrines drew down the sentence of excommunication, and led to a serious feud, in which Kimchi appeared as the friend of Maimonides, and endeavoured to make peace. In the course of time, however, the opinions of all gained ground, and have now an almost universal influence on Jewish habits of thought, which makes a knowledge of their writings desirable.

A specimen of Kimchi's Commentary is now presented to the public, as a small contribution towards this object. It is hoped that even this may be useful, not only in exhibiting Jewish interpretation, but in helping Christians to form a more correct estimate of the Jewish mind. The controversialist is compelled to attack that which is erroneous, or even absurd in the oral law, and the ignorant or unthinking hastily conclude that all the Jewish writings are of the same character. The translation of Kimchi or Aben Ezra would speedily undeceive the world. In the mean while it is hoped that the patient reader of even this specimen, will rise with a different idea of Jewish talent and learning. It may also facilitate the study of Rabbinical literature to some who have commenced, and induce others to begin. The controversy with the Jews is an important branch of Christian divinity, which is comparatively overlooked, and cannot be effectually cultivated without some knowledge of the rabbies. It was principally for the conversion of the Jews, that the oriental professorships were determined on at the Council of Vienna, in 1311,* and it is to be hoped that those who appreciate the value of Christianity now, will also remember that this is one use of knowing the original language of the Old Testament. To those whose other avocations do not permit them to study Rabbinical writers this translation may prove useful, especially as constant regard has been had to the Jewish controversies, and the chief passages relating to the Messiah have been considered, somewhat at length, in observations appended to the chapters in which they occur.

The present translation was made from the text in Buxtorf's Bible, but it is much to be wished that one of the Universities would furnish students with a more correct and cheaper edition. Wolfius mentions that this portion of Kimchi was translated into Latin by Robert

* Gesen. Geschichte, p. 104.

Neal, and published in Paris in 1577, but I have never had the good fortune to see it, or I should have gladly availed myself of its assistance. Buxtorf's text has been compared, so far as that abridgement will allow, with Solomon Ben Melech's מכלל יופי Perfection of Beauty, and the passages of the Talmud, &c., cited by Kimchi, are pointed out in the notes. Should this specimen of Rabbinic comment be approved by students, the Translator hopes, at some future period, to present them with another. The next would probably be Saadiah Gaon's Commentary on the Book of Daniel, of parts of which he has had a translation lying by for some years. His wish, however, would be, in course of time, to furnish Kimchi's Commentary on the Prophets complete, with observations on all the passages relating to the Messiah. There is in English no book that fully considers the Jewish objections, and to meet this want the Translator originally intended an English translation of the Chizzuk Emunah, with notes. But on considering that a large part of that book is occupied with objections common to all who reject the New Testament, and which have, therefore, been answered already elsewhere; and that his interpretation of the prophecies are drawn chiefly from Kimchi, he thought that the Commentary of the original objector would be more useful. But, perhaps, he was influenced still more by the consideration that the magnitude of a detailed answer to the Chizzuk Emunah would make the undertaking too great a pecuniary risk.

KIMCHI'S

COMMENTARY ON ZECHARIAH.

CHAPTER I.

1 "*In the eighth month, in the second year of Darius, was the word of the Lord unto Zechariah, the son of Berechiah, the son of Iddo, the prophet, saying.*"

"*The prophet,*" is to be referred to Zechariah, though perhaps Iddo may also have been a prophet, for it is said that he is the same as Iddo, the seer. (2 Chron. ix. 29.) We have also found in the Midrash* the words, "Iddo, the prophet."

"*Saying,*" to Israel, as is immediately added, "And thou shalt say unto them." Say unto them, that they should remember the displeasure wherewith the Lord was displeased with the fathers, that is, with the generation in whose time the temple was desolated; they should also remember that it was on account of their deeds that the Lord was displeased with them, they should therefore return to the Lord, and not be like their fathers. They were at this time slothful in building the temple, for they did not begin to build until the ninth month, and evil deeds were still in their hands, as is written in the book of Ezra.

* Medrash, or Midrash, is the title of several compilations of traditional expositions of the Scripture. The most famous are the Midrash Rabba on the Pentateuch, Esther, Lamentations, &c., and the Midrash Tillim on the Psalms.

3. "*Therefore say.*"—This is plain.

4. "*Be not.*"—This is plain.

5. "*Your fathers, where are they?*"—Do ye not see that they have been consumed by the sword, the famine, and the pestilence, as the prophets said to them?

"*And the prophets, do they live for ever?*" The prophets, who reproved them, could they live for ever, and reprove them? He reproved them already, and they did not hearken. But see how every thing has happened to them, as the prophets announced, and as is said (in the following verse), "But my words and statutes," &c. Our Rabbies, of blessed memory, have interpreted * the words, "The prophets, where are they," as the answer of the people. They say that the congregation of Israel gave a controversial reply to the prophet. He said to them, Return in true repentance, for your fathers sinned, and where are they? The people answered him, And the prophets who did not sin, where are they? But they afterwards repented and made confession to him.

6. "*But my words and statutes.*"—My statutes, i. e. my evil decrees which I decreed concerning them, that they should die by the sword, and by famine, and by pestilence, and that the survivors should be led away captive, do ye not see that they have overtaken your fathers, and have all come upon them, as I commanded my servants the prophets to announce to them? and they themselves repented and confessed this in the time of the desolation, as is said in the following verse, "And they returned and said."

7. "*Upon the four and twentieth day of the eleventh month,*" that is, the month Shevat.—As to the names of the months, as they are written in the roll of Esther, and in this book we do not know whether they are Chaldee or not, for we do not find them in the other holy books.

"*The word of the Lord was to Zechariah.*"—An angel

* In the Talm. Bab. Sanhedrin, fol. 105. 1.

came to him, and spake with him, and showed him this vision, which he is now narrating.

8. "*I saw by night.*"—The visions of Zechariah are very obscure, like those of Daniel, but the visions of the other prophets are not so; the reason is, that the power of prophecy had been gradually exhausting from the days of the captivity; therefore, they did not make their words clear, and did not understand the visions as they were. He says, "I saw by night," i. e., in the visions of the night I saw this vision, in which I beheld "a man riding upon a red horse." We have found in the words * of our rabbies of blessed memory, the following exposition of this verse:—"I saw in the night, that the Holy One, blessed be He, sought to turn the whole world into night, and behold a man riding. This man is no other than the Holy One, blessed be He, for it is said, 'The Lord is a man of war.' † 'Upon a red horse.' The Holy One, blessed be He, sought to turn the whole world into blood, but when he looked upon Hannaniah, Mishael, and Azariah, his anger was cooled, for it is said, 'And he stood among the myrtle-trees, הֲדַסִּים. (hadassim.') The myrtle-trees can mean nothing else but the righteous, for it is said, 'He brought up Hadassah.' ‡ (Esther ii. 7.) In like manner, 'In the bottom,' בַּמְּצֻלָה, means nothing else but Babylon, for it is said, 'That saith to the deep, צוּלָה, be dry.' (Isaiah xliv. 27.) Immediately the black horses became speckled, and the red horses white, for it is said, 'And behind him red horses, speckled and white.' (Verse 8.)" But we shall endeavour to interpret the vision as well as we can.

* Talm. Bab. Sanhedrin, fol. 93, col. 1.

† This is a remarkable testimony to the belief of the ancient Jews, that He, who appeared in the form of a man, as the angel of the Lord, was the God of Israel.

‡ Esther's name was Hadassah, a myrtle-tree, and as she was righteous, the rabbies conclude that "myrtle-trees" in Zechariah, also stands for righteous persons.

"*A man.*"—That is, the angel of the Lord, as in Dan. ix. 21, "The man Gabriel;" and so we read further on, "The angel of the Lord that stood between the myrtle-trees." He saw him riding upon a horse, to denote his speed in embassy. As to the meaning of the word "red," and the other colours, it may be that some definite meaning was intended by them; and my lord my father, of blessed memory, has written, that the *red horse* is typical of Nebuchadnezzar, who is called the head of gold, and gold is red; for this prophecy refers to the four kingdoms, like the dream of Nebuchadnezzar, and the visions of Daniel. And although the horses figuratively represent the angels the messengers of God, there is, nevertheless, a reference to the four kingdoms. The vision of "a man riding," signifies that the angels rule over the lower world, and that all the work of God on earth is done by them and through their mediation. The object of the man's mission was to root up the kingdom of Babylon; and although at the time of this vision the Babylonian monarchy had been already rooted out, the vision was exhibited to him complete, as it had been, on account of the three kingdoms that were still future. The vision happened in the time of the Persian monarchy, as is said, "In the second year of Darius."

"*And he stood amongst the myrtle-trees that were in the bottom.*"—These signify Israel, and he compares them to myrtle-trees; for as these have a good odour, so the Israelites in Babylon had the good odour of the commandments. He is represented as standing among them to help them, and deliver them from captivity.

"*In the bottom.*"—This is Babylon.

"*And behind him red horses, speckled and white.*"—"Speckled," a species of colour, but what colour is not clear to us. There are some who say, that it means, coloured with colouring stuff, but this is nonsense. The speckled horses in this vision, are instead of the black horses in the other vision of the four chariots. (Chap. vi.) The Targum of Jonathan renders "speckled" by סחתין, and according to another reading, קווחין, "bay."* So far as appears, these horses had no riders upon them: he that was riding was the prince or captain over the other angels, and therefore he saw him riding. "*And behind him red horses.*"—If we interpret "a red horse," of Nebuchadnezzar, then we should interpret the "red horses," of his son and grandson; and, behold! these answer to the first chariot (in chap. vi.). "*Speckled and white.*" As if he had said, Behind them were speckled horses, and behind them again white. And, behold! he does not mention any thing to answer to the fourth chariot, for he did not see it in this vision, on account of its distance, but in the other vision he did see it.

9. "*And I said ——— he that spake with me, said.*" —This answers to what is said above, "The word of the Lord was to Zechariah."

"*I will show thee*" (literally, I will cause thee to see). —He ought to have said, I will cause thee to hear, for he did not show him any thing more than the vision of the horses, which he had shown him from the beginning. "I will show thee," may mean, I will cause thee to hear; for the sense of seeing is employed figuratively for the other senses, as it is said, "And all the people saw the thunderings." (Exod. xx. 18.) "See the smell of my son." (Gen. xxvii. 27.) But the literal interpretation of "I will show thee," is also good, for it may refer to the other vision of the four horns, which is clearer than this, though he did not understand it until it was explained to him.

10. "*And he answered.*" He that was riding upon the horse.—The prophet heard the angel riding on the horse answer, although he had not asked him any thing; and he said to him, These horses are the messengers of God,

* This is the present reading.

whom he hath sent to walk to and fro through the earth, in the same way as Satan said, "From going to and fro in the earth, and from walking up and down in it." (Job i. 7.) But, perhaps, the angel that was riding, did not answer the prophet at all, but the word "answer," is to be taken, as in Deut. xxvi. 5, "Thou shalt answer, and say;" and again, in Job iii. 2, "And Job answered and said," where it occurs the first time. And then the sense may be, that the prophet heard the rider on the horse speaking to, and asking those horses, which the Lord had sent to walk to and fro through the earth, what was the state of the earth:* and they answered and said, "We have walked to and fro through the earth, and have seen it sitting still, and at rest." "These," may signify "to these;" and thus (the preposition is omitted in the following cases), "One told David, saying, Ahitophel is among the conspirators." Here David is the same as "to David." (2 Sam. xv. 31.) And again, "And two men, captains of bands, were the son of Saul," i. e., to the son of Saul; and there are other similar passages.

11. "*And they answered.*"—This is plain.

"*Sitteth still, and is at rest,*" i. e., We have seen the peace of the Gentile nations, and Israel in trouble, therefore the angel answered and said, "How long wilt thou not have mercy upon Jerusalem?"

12. *And the angel of the Lord answered,*" i. e., either he who was standing among the myrtle-trees, who was for the help of Israel, or the angel that was speaking

* Kimchi thinks, for certain reasons which he immediately subjoins, that the Hebrew words may also be translated thus, "The man that stood between the myrtle-trees answered and said to those whom the Lord sent forth to walk through the earth." But though he shows that, in some other cases, the preposition "to" is omitted, this translation cannot be justified; first, because the Athnach under וַיֹּאמַר separates it from אֵלֶּה; and, secondly, because after the verb אָמַר, the words spoken almost always follow, which is not the case here.

with the prophet; and this last is the true (interpretation).*

"*How long wilt thou not have mercy upon Jerusalem?*"—As long as the Gentile nations are at rest, (Israel) cannot go forth from captivity, nor, until the destruction of Babylon. And, behold! the subject of this vision was long past at the time when he saw it; but the angel shows him the past, in order to let him see that the prosperity of Babylon and its desolation were all from God, blessed be He, through the mediation of the conducting angels,† and that they were employed in promoting the welfare of Israel; and that the three remaining kingdoms and their fall should also be from God, according to what he had shown him of the Babylonian monarchy, which was past.

"*Against which thou hast had just indignation these threescore and ten years.*"—If these words refer to the past, as we have interpreted, then the seventy years refer to the kingdom of Babylon, and the indignation was that which existed during the whole time of Nebuchadnezzar. Or, the seventy years may have been mentioned in reference to the time of the vision, which was in the second year of Darius; at which time the seventy years were complete for the desolation of Jerusalem. For although this vision was in the month Shevat,‡ and they had begun to build in Kislev,§ nevertheless the indignation still continued, and during all the time of the building the city, they were at war with their enemies.

* Kimchi is here wrong in supposing that the angel who spake with Zechariah is called "the angel of the Lord." But this interpretation, though wrong, is very important, as showing Kimchi's decided opinion, that the angel who stood among the myrtle-trees, is not identical with the angelus interpres who speaks with him. (Compare Hengsbenberg's Christologie, part ii., p. 22.)

† Compare what is said in verse 8, and also chap. ii. 3, and the note.

‡ About our January.

§ About our November.

13. "*And the Lord answered .... words, comforts,*" דְּבָרִים נִחֻמִּים.—The governing word is omitted. The absolute form דְּבָרִים, is to be interpreted as if it were דִּבְרֵי נִחֻמִּים, "words of comfort;" or נִחֻמִּים may be an adjective, and this is the fact.*

14. "*And the angel said to me.*"—The good words which God, blessed be He, spake to him, he spake to me, that I might proclaim them in the ears of Israel to comfort them.

15. "*I am sore displeased* —— *heathen at ease,*" that is, as is said above, "Sitteth still, and is at rest."

"*I was a little displeased.*"—I was a little displeased with Israel, so as to carry them captive from their land, and this word, a "little," is put in contrast to what they (the Gentiles) had done to Israel after their captivity.

"*Helped forward the affliction*" by doing them evil, more than enough, and so it is said in Isaiah, "I was wroth with my people, I profaned my inheritance, and delivered them into thy hand, but thou showedst them no mercy; upon the ancient hast thou heavily laid thy yoke." (Isaiah xlvii. 6.)

16. "*Therefore thus saith the Lord*" —— and a line וְקָוה, the Kethib has a ה at the end, like נָוֶה (a dwelling). The Keri is without the ה (קָו). The word signifies a building line, a cord, which they stretch over the row of bricks.

17. "*Cry yet* —— *through good shall be spread abroad.*"—On account of the abundance of good and prosperity that they shall have, they shall be spread abroad; that is to say, the inhabited part shall increase. וְנִחַם has pathach, and is from a dageshed conjugation.†

* And so our translators have rendered it. Michaelis, in the notes to his Hebrew Bible, leaves the matter doubtful. Gesenius, in his Lexicon, decides that נִחֻמִּים is a substantive, and refers to Isaiah lvii. 18; וַאֲשַׁלֵּם נִחֻמִים לוֹ, "And I will restore comforts unto him." To which opinion Rosenmüller also subscribes in his Scholia. The Septuagint agrees with Kimchi and the English; it has Λόγους παρακλητικούς.

† It is Pihel.

OBSERVATIONS ON CHAPTER I.

מלאך יהוה, The Angel, or Messenger of the Lord.

From Kimchi's commentary on the 8th and 12th verses of this chapter, it appears that he considered the person designated "The angel of the Lord," as nothing more than one of the many angels to whom he supposes that the governance and guidance of this lower world is committed. It has been repeatedly proved by Christian writers that this Being is none other than the Son of God. The latest writers in this country are Mr. Faber in his "Horæ Mosaicæ,"* and Dr. Pye Smith, in his work on the Messiah; but as their works were not written with a special reference to the Jewish controversy, and as the question is one of general importance, it may not be out of place to offer a few remarks on the character of the angel or messenger of the Lord.

Kimchi evidently took the word מַלְאָךְ, as signifying "angel," and therefore decides that he is one of that class of heavenly beings commonly designated by that name. But the first and original meaning of the word is "messenger," in which sense it is frequently applied to men as well as to heavenly beings. In Gen. xxxii. 1. 3 (Heb. ii. 4) it occurs in both senses. "And Jacob went on his way, and the angels of God, מַלְאֲכֵי אֱלֹהִים, met him." "And Jacob sent messengers, מַלְאָכִים, before him to Esau his brother." The word itself, therefore, decides nothing as to the nature of the messenger; so far as that is concerned, he may be a man, or he may be a heavenly being, but if a heavenly being, it decides nothing as to the order to which he belongs, whether to the living creatures de-

* Not having access to this work, I cannot give the reference. Dr. Pye Smith treats this subject in vol. i. pp. 333.

scribed in Ezekiel, or to the Seraphim mentioned in Isaiah, or to others.

The next question is, How are the two words מַלְאַךְ יְהוָֹה, to be translated? Some Christians wish to translate "The angel Jehovah." But this is plainly against the punctuation, and if persons pretend to disregard the points, then we must add against the consonants also. If the two words are to be taken in apposition, without regard to the points, the translation must be "An angel or a messenger, Jehovah." If מַלְאָךְ were used in the absolute form with reference to THE LORD, we should expect that it would have the article ה before it, as אָדוֹן has uniformly, so that the form הָאָדוֹן, the Lord, is never applied to any created being. Besides, the words do occur in Scripture elsewhere, where יְהוָֹה must be taken as the genitive case, as "The priest's lips should keep knowledge, and they should seek the law at his mouth, כִּי מַלְאַךְ יְהוָֹה־צְבָאוֹת הוּא, for he is the messenger of the Lord of Hosts." (Mal. iii. 7.)

The modern Jews, on the other hand, translate "An angel of the Lord," and in this our translators have occasionally followed them, as in Judges ii. 1, "An angel of the Lord, מלאך יהוה, came up from Gilgal:" but there is nothing in the words to compel us to adopt this translation. As far as they are concerned, we may with equal propriety translate "The angel of the Lord." It cannot be urged that מַלְאַךְ has not got the article, for it is in regimen, and the general rule is, that nouns in regimen do not take the article, but are made definite by the following genitive, and the Jews themselves will admit that אֱלֹהֵי יִשְׂרָאֵל must be translated "The God of Israel;" and הַר הַבַּיִת, "The mountain of the house;' הֵיכַל יְהוָֹה, "The temple of the Lord." It is true that in this case the general rule is, that the definite article should be prefixed to the genitive; but here that cannot be the case, for יְהוָֹה never, in any case, receives an article. Suppose, then, that the sacred writers wished to express that מַלְאַךְ יְהוָה is to be translated definitely, "The angel of the Lord," what means could they have taken? They could not have put the article before מַלְאַךְ, for that would have made "The angel Jehovah." They could not prefix it to יְהוָה, for, as we have said, that does not admit of it. There remained one other course possible, and that was, never to use the expression in the plural of angels, but always in the singular, so as to indicate that one person, and one only, is intended. But have they done this? Yes, uniformly: in the whole Bible, and in the great variety of styles which occurs, we never once find the expression מַלְאֲכֵי יְהוָה, "Angels of the Lord," but uniformly the singular, מַלְאַךְ יְהוָה, to point out that there is only one of heavenly beings to whom this title belongs. It would be folly, or something worse, to say that this is fortuitous. The uniformity of the practice by all the sacred writers implies design, and teaches that there is but one person thus called, and that therefore the true translation is, "The angel of the Lord."

The only plausible objection that can be urged is, that though we do not find in the plural "The angels of the Lord," we do find the expression, "Angels of God." We might urge in reply, that there is a great difference between the words אלהים and יהוה, but this is not necessary, as this very objection will serve as an additional confirmation to the foregoing argument. We have already said, that a word governing a genitive case does not take the article, and that the rule therefore is, if the article is wanted, to prefix it to the genitive case, if the genitive be a word that admits of the article. Now אֱלֹהִים is a word that admits the article. When, therefore, the sacred writers wished to say definitely "The angel of God," they could express it by מַלְאַךְ הָאֱלֹהִים, and this they have done, as in Gen. xxxi. 11, "And the angel of God, מַלְאַךְ הָאֱלֹהִים, spake unto me in a dream." And again, in Exod. xiv. 19, "And the angel of God, מַלְאַךְ הָאֱלֹהִים, which went before the camp," &c.; and so in very many other cases. As, therefore, when they wished to use a definite expression, they had it in their power, it was not necessary to confine the expression, "Angel of God," to the singular. But now mark the care and accuracy of the sacred writers; when they use angels of God in the plural, they do not use the article before אֱלֹהִים: that is, they do not make it definite. It occurs only twice in the Bible, but each time without the article. First, in Jacob's dream of the ladder, "And, behold, angels of God מַלְאֲכֵי אֱלֹהִים, ascending and descending on it." (Genesis xxviii. 12.) And again in the instance quoted above, "And Jacob went on his way, and angels of God, מַלְאֲכֵי אֱלֹהִים, met him." (Genesis xxxii. 1, Hebrew 2.) This expression, therefore, "Angels of God," is so far from weakening our former argument, that it shows us that there is one peculiar being, who is distinguished from all other heavenly beings, by the title, "The angel of the Lord;" and that, therefore, the analogy of Scripture confirms us in the faith, that there is only one person who is called "The angel of the Lord."

It may be thought needful to prove that He who is called "The angel of the Lord," is identical with him who is named "The angel of God;" but this is easily done. In Judges vi. 20, 21, we find both expressions indifferently applied to one and the same person. "And *the angel of God* said unto him, Take the flesh and the unleavened cakes, and lay them upon this rock, and pour the broth. And he did so. Then *the angel of the Lord* put forth the end of his staff," &c. And again, Judges xiii. 3—9, "And *the angel of the Lord* appeared unto the woman———And God hearkened to the voice of Manoah; and *the angel of God* came again unto the woman." Here the identity is fully proved, and we have got thus far in our inquiry, that there is but one heavenly being who is called "The angel of the Lord" and "The angel of God," and consequently that He is some way peculiar from those other heavenly beings, who have not these titles, but are called "Angels of God." Wherein that peculiarity consists, we now proceed to inquire.

It is not possible in the limited space, to which we propose to extend these observations, to go through all the passages on this subject, we, therefore, select a few plain ones, sufficient to establish what is advanced. The first peculiarity, then, in the character of this personage is, that he is called by the proper name of God, יְהוָה. We read in the law, that He appeared to Hagar, when she fled from her mistress; and after relating the vision, the the sacred history adds, "And she called the name of the Lord, יהוה, who spake with her," so that He who was before called the angel of the Lord, is here called Jehovah. Rashi, Aben Ezra, Solomon ben Melech, and Nachmanides, all pass this over in silence. Individual Jews to whom I have proposed the passage, have almost always replied, that Hagar was mistaken, and from ignorance applied the name Jehovah to the angel. But this is not the fact, Hagar did not call the angel Jehovah; she called him אֵל רָאִי, or as our translation has it, "Thou God seest me." It is the historian, in the course of his narrative, who applies to the angel the name Jehovah, and this is acknowledged by Abarbanel, who says that this is an exceedingly difficult passage, particularly "Because the peculiar name of God is employed, 'She called the name of the Lord who spake with her;' and how can it possibly be, that the First Cause, blessed be He, should speak with Hagar; when the law itself testifies and says, that it was the angel of the Lord who appeared unto her, and not the Lord himself?" A little lower down He gives his solution of the difficulty thus; "The right answer here is, that all prophetic vision, whether mediate or immediate, is always attributed to God, blessed be He, for it is from Him and by His will, and on this account also the Messenger is sometimes called by the name of Him that sends him. In this point of view it is that the Scripture here says, 'And she called the name of the LORD that spake to her.'" (Abarbanel in loc.)* His solution we shall consider presently; but now only remark that he admits that the angel of the Lord is here called Jehovah, and proceed

To take a similar instance from the historical books. In the Book of Judges, vi. 11, we read that the angel of the Lord appeared to Gideon. At verse 14, we suddenly find this person called Jehovah the LORD. "And the LORD, יהוה, looked upon him, and said, Go in this thy might." And again, verse 16, "And the LORD, יהוה said unto him, Surely I will be with thee." We refer to this passage, because the fact is admitted by the rabbies. Kimchi says, in his Commentary on the last quoted verse, "In the words, 'The LORD said unto him,' the angel is called by the name of the Lord, as is the case also with the angel who appeared to Joshua, of whom it is written, 'And the LORD, יהוה, said unto Joshua.'" (Josh. vi. 2.)† And in this passage of Joshua to which he refers, he says, "And the Lord said unto Joshua, that is, through the angel who appeared to him, and he is called by the name of the LORD who sent him. And we find a similar instance in the angel who appeared to Gideon, of whom it is written, 'And the Lord said unto him, Surely, I will be with thee.' Our rabbies of blessed memory have said, 'My name is in him.' R. Simeon ben Lakish says, 'This teaches us, that the Holy One, blessed be He, associates his name to each of the angels."‡ We

* Edit. Venice, 1584, fol. 61, col. 4.

† ומה שאמר ויאמר אליו יי׳ קרא המלאך בשם יי׳ כמו שכתוב במלאך שנראה ליהושע ויאמר יי׳ ליהושע ׃

‡ ויאמר יי׳ אל יהושע ע״י המלאך הנראה לו והוא נקרא בשם יי׳ השולח אותו וכן

have here the same admission made, and the same solution proposed, as in the former case by Abarbanel.

We now take a similar instance from the prophets. In the third chapter of Zechariah, Joshua the high-priest, is represented as standing before the angel of the Lord, and then it is added, "And the LORD, יהוה, said unto Satan, The Lord rebuke thee, O Satan." The person called in the first verse the angel of the Lord, is in the second verse called the LORD, as Kimchi himself acknowledges; "This is said of the angel, who is called by the name of his master, and so in the history of Gideon, and other places."

From these three passages, selected from the law, the historical books, and the Prophets, it appears, that the Being designated by the title "The angel of the Lord," is also called יהוה, Jehovah, the proper name of God; and from the Rabbinical Commentaries it appears, that this inference is not peculiar to Christians, nor forced from the text in order to suit their doctrinal views, but that those rabbies who made it their peculiar care to overthrow every interpretation favourable to Christianity, were nevertheless constrained by the plainness and frequency of such passages, to come to the same conclusion. They did not make this admission in ignorance, they evidently foresaw the use that would be made of it, and, therefore, endeavour to guard against it by saying, "that the messenger is called by the name of Him that sends him." But this explanation, taken as a general assertion, is, in the first place, contrary to fact. In the eighth and ninth chapters of Daniel, an angel is sent to Daniel, but he is not called by the name of Him that sent him, but is called Gabriel. In the prophecies of Zechariah we read of many angels of whom it is said, "These are they

מצאנו במלאך שנראה לגדעון ויאמר אליו י״ כי אהיה עמך ויאמרו רז״ל כי שמי בקרבו אר״ שמעון בן לקיש מלמד שהק״בה משתף שמו על כל מלאך ומלאך ·

whom the Lord hath sent to walk to and fro through the earth," but they are not called by the name of their Lord. In like manner Isaiah saw an angel sent to him to remove his iniquity, but this angel is not called by the name of his master, but "one of the Seraphim." In the second place, if taken with special reference to the particular case of the angel of the Lord, this explanation is no explanation at all, but a mere identical proposition in somewhat different words. When I say the angel of the Lord is called Jehovah, what else is intended but this, "That the messenger is called by the name of Him that sends him?" This last sentence is, therefore, no explanation of the first, and still less a removal of the difficulty. The difficulty is, why, for what reasons is the Messenger called by the name of Him who sends him? If this were the universal practice, if every angel were called Jehovah, we might say, it is the style of Scripture to ascribe the peculiar name of God to all his messengers, but this cannot be pretended. There are many instances where the angels have no names, and others, where a peculiar name is ascribed; the question then is, Why is the angel of the Lord called by His name? And this question acquires double force from what we have proved above, that there is but one Being who is called the Angel of the Lord, or *The* Angel of God. Why, then, is this one individual called by that august name, Jehovah, and the others not? And, observe, that it has not only been proved from the Scripture that the name Jehovah is ascribed to only one angel, but that it can be proved also that this was the opinion of the ancient Jews. The Talmud has the following passage, "The same heretic said to Rav Idith, It is written, 'And he said unto Moses, Come up unto the LORD' (Exod. xxiv. 1), but it ought to have been written, 'Come up unto me.' The rabbi answered, The speaker here is Metatron, whose name is the same as that of his master, for it is written, 'For my name is in him.' (Exod. xxiii. 21.)" * This passage is obviously the source whence Kimchi and Abarbanel borrowed the above explanation, but here the explanation is not general, applying to all angels, but only to one, whose name is Metatron. And the occasion of this reply plainly shows that the other opinion, that the name Jehovah is ascribed indiscriminately to all angels was then unknown, for, if it had been, it would have been a more plausible answer to the heretic's objection. The real difficulty, therefore, remains in all its force, why is the peculiar and proper name of God applied to the angel of the Lord?

That there is in the name יהוה, Jehovah, a peculiarity which distinguishes it from all the other names of God, is expressly asserted by God himself, and is the uniform doctrine both of Jews and Christians. God says,

אֲנִי יְהוָה הוּא שְׁמִי

"I am Jehovah; that is my name: and my glory will I not give to another, neither my praise to graven images" (Isaiah xlii. 8); which Kimchi thus paraphrases, "That is my name, which is appropriated to myself alone, not like the name of the graven images; for although their worshippers associate them with me in the application of the name אֱלֹהִים, God, they cannot associate them with me in this name; for I am Lord over all." † Again we read in Hosea xii. 5, (Heb. 6),

וַיהוָה אֱלֹהֵי הַצְּבָאוֹת יְהוָה זִכְרוֹ

"Even Jehovah the God of Hosts; Jehovah is his memorial." Upon which passage Kimchi speaks still more decidedly in the following words: "Although he

* אמר ההוא מינא לרב אידית כתיב ואל משה אמר עלה אל ה׳ עלה אלי מיבעי ליה א״ל זהו מטטרון ששמו כשם רבו דכתיב כי שמי בקרבו :—Sanhedrim, fol. 38, col. 2.

† הוא שמי המיוחד לי לא כשם הפסילים אף על פי שעובדיהם ישתתפו אותם עמי בשם אלהי׳ ולא יוכלו לשתפם עמי הזה השם כי אני הוא אדון על הכל ·

was revealed to your fathers in the name God Almighty, saying to him, 'I am God Almighty, increase and multiply' (Gen. xxxv. 11); yet to Moses he renewed his fearful name, and all this for your sakes, by means of it to renew signs and wonders, to bring you forth from slavery to liberty, and this new name is Jehovah, יהוה, and he is the God of Hosts. God of Hosts expresses that degree, in which stand the angels, and the orbs with their stars, for in the names אֵל and אֱלֹהִים, he (God) is associated with them; but in this name He is associated with none but himself."* These two passages show that Jehovah is the proper name of God, and that this was Kimchi's decided opinion. His Comment on the last passage shows, how little he believed in his own explanation, "that the messenger is called by the name of Him that sends him," for he plainly says, that in the name Jehovah God has no partner whatever. But this opinion is not peculiar to Kimchi, it is the ancient and received Jewish doctrine. In the first place, it is the opinion of the Talmud, where on the verse, "On this wise shall ye bless the children of Israel," it is said, that is, with the name Jehovah. If you object, that it may be with the name Jehovah, or it may not be, but with the cognomen Lord; the objection is answered by the following words, 'And they shall put my name.' (Numb. vi. 27.) My name, the name that is appropriated to me alone."†

In like manner the book of Kosri, "The Deity is called אֱלֹהִים in genere, but is called Jehovah in his individuality; for if any one should ask, What God ought we to worship? the sun, or the moon, or the heavens, or the constellations, or one of the stars, or the fire, or the

* אע״פי שנגלה לאביכם באל שדי לאמר לו אני אל שדי פרה ורבה עוד חדש שמו הנכבד למשה והכל בעבורכם לחדש בו אותות ומופתים להוציאכם מעבדות לחירית והוא י״וד ה״א יו״ד ה״א והוא אלהי הצבאת אלהי צבאות מעלה שהם המלאכים והגלגלים עם כוכביהם ובשם אל ואלהי׳ הוא משתתף עמהם אבל בזה השם אינו משתתף עם זולתו ׃

† כן הברכו את בני ישראל בשם מפורש אתה אומר בשם מפורש או אינו אלא בכנוי ת״ל ושמו את שמי שמי המיוחד לי וגו׳—Sotah. fol. 38. 1.

wind, or the spiritual angels, for each of these has a certain work and dominion, and each of them is a cause in existence and in destruction? The answer would be, Jehovah, just as you call a certain person by a known name, as Reuben, Simeon, &c."* Maimonides devotes a whole chapter to the discussion of this one point, from which we quote as follows: "All the names of God which occur in Scripture are all derived from the works, as is well known, except one name, and that is, יהוה, which is the name appropriated to God alone. And this is called the plain name (Shem hammephorash), because it teaches plainly and unequivocally of the substance of God." † "The sum of the whole matter is, the dignity of this name, and the prohibition to read it, is to be ascribed to this, that it points directly to the substance of God, and on this account, not one of the creatures has a share in the teaching of this name, as our rabbies of blessed memory have said: 'My name, the name that is appropriated to me alone.'" The author of the Kosri and Maimonides were controversialists, and had the Christian controversy constantly in view, their testimony is, therefore, doubly valuable; and when we combine the admissions of opponents with the plain words of Scripture, there can be no doubt of these two things, first, that the name Jehovah is the peculiar name of God; and, secondly, that God has claimed it for himself, because it has reference to that substance and essence peculiar to himself. Why, then, is it communicated to the angel of the Lord? There can be but one answer: because He partakes of that substance and essence which makes the communication of the name suitable; or, in other words, because the angel of the Lord is very God. And this conclusion is confirmed

By the second peculiarity in the Scripture delineation of his character, and that is, that He not only has the

* Part iv. 1. Buxtorf's edition, page 257, 258.

† Part i. cap. 61.

incommunicable name of God, but is represented as having the divine nature, and as being the God of Abraham, Isaac, and Jacob.

The first proof to be adduced on this subject, is from the xxxist chapter of Genesis. The angel of God, מַלְאַךְ הָאֱלֹהִים, appeared to Jacob in a dream, and said to him, "I am the God of Bethel, where thou anointedst the pillar, and where thou vowedst a vow unto me." (Gen. xxxi. 13.) Here this Being first says of himself, "I am the God of Bethel." Some modern Jews may and do quibble about the word אֵל; we shall not, therefore, in this short Essay, enter into that question, and the rather as it is here unnecessary. The angel not only says that He is God, but that Jacob had worshipped him as such; "Where thou anointedst the pillar, and where thou vowedst the vow TO ME." Then beyond all doubt He was God, the true object of worship, for if Jacob had made a mistake, neither the angel nor the sacred historian would have passed by the sin of idolatry unnoticed and unreproved. Besides, if we turn to the passage relating to the circumstance of this vow, we find that it was made to the God of his fathers: "The Lord stood above the ladder, and said, I am the God of Abraham, thy father, and the God of Isaac." (Gen. xxviii. 13.) If, then, the Scripture is to be taken in its plain grammatical sense, this angel was the God of Bethel, the God of Abraham, and Isaac, and the God whom Jacob worshipped, and to whom he vowed the vow.

But now let us hear the rabbies. Rashi and Aben Ezra pass the passage without remarking on the nature of the angel. Ramban * says, "The angel speaks in the name of Him that sent him, but this angel might truly say, 'I am the God of Bethel;' for it is said in like manner, 'He called the place El Bethel, the God of

* R. Moses ben Nachman, commonly called by Christian writers Nachmanides.

Bethel' (Gen. xxxv. 7), according as it is said, 'Zion, the Holy One of Israel.' (Isa. lx. 14.) But Jonathan, the son of Uzziel says, The Holy One, in the heavens of the highest height, the house of his Shechinah, and this is 'the angel the Redeemer;' and in like manner it is written, 'Who is faithful in all my house.' (Numb. xii. 7.) The wise will understand." * (Comment. in loc.) Nachmanides here gives two interpretations; first, he says, that he is called the God of Bethel, because He is the messenger of the God of Bethel, but this is a pure assertion, without any proof, as we have seen above. Secondly, he says, that he may have this title in truth, just as the place was called the God of Bethel, and as Zion is called the Holy One of Israel. If this be taken to mean, that this angel was no more God than Bethel itself was, this explanation will not solve the difficulty, for it is said, not only that He was called God, but that he was worshipped as God, which is not said either of Bethel or of Zion, so that the passages are not parallel; and further, the instance from Isaiah rests upon a false translation. Zion, ציון, is feminine, as may be seen in Isaiah i. 2, so that ציון קדוש ישראל, cannot be translated otherwise than it is in the English translation. But it may well be doubted whether this was his meaning. Nachmanides was a cabbalist, and most probably alluded to the mystical interpretation of Beth (house) in the words, El Bethel, as he certainly does, when he quotes the words, "Who was faithful in all my house." He did not choose to speak plainly, and therefore says, "The wise will understand:" and this supposition will be much confirmed by the very similar comment of Bechai, which shall be given presently. But whether this supposition be founded or not, it is plain

* והמלאך ידבר בלשון שולחו ועל דרך האמת אמר המלאך הזה אנכי האל בית אל וכן ויקרא למקום אל בית אל. כמו שאמר ציון קדוש ישראל ויונתן בן עוזיאל אמר קדיש בשמי מרומא עילאה בית שכינתיה והוא מלאך הגואל. וכן בכל בתי נאמן הוא והמשכיל יבין ·

that Nachmanides considered the words, "I am the God of Bethel, &c.," as applying to the angel.

Bechai says, "If interpreted literally, the words, 'I am the God of Bethel,' mean, The God that appeared to thee in Bethel. But according to cabbalistic interpretation, this angel who calls himself the God of Bethel, is the goodness spoken of in the words, 'I will make all my goodness pass before thee' (Exod. xxxiii. 19), and he is the house mentioned in the words, 'Who was faithful in all my house,' for a man's goodness is his house, and, therefore, he says of himself, I am the God of Bethel. And so it is said of Jacob, 'He called the place El Bethel.' But, behold, even according to the literal interpretation of the verse, it is certain that this angel is the God of Bethel, and understand this."* (Comment. in loc.) Bechai also fully agrees to the fact that the angel is called the God of Bethel, and the reasons which he assigns, evidently point to the Shechinah or habitation which he calls "The house;" and, further, "The goodness of the Lord;" so that from this Commentary it would appear that the Shechinah is the Being here alluded to.

In the Commentary of Menachem of Rekanata, the same opinion is expressed still more clearly. He says, "The angel mentioned above, said to him, I am the God of Bethel, by which is intended the Shechinah, who is called angel, for she † appeared to the fathers, and to her the vow was made, and, therefore, it is said, Where thou vowedst the vow to me, as is explained above. She is called angel, because the government of this world is by her mouth. And understand that she is called

* אנכי האל בית אל · ע"ד הפשט שנגלה לך בבי' אל · וע"ד הקבל' המלאך הזה שקרא עצמו אל הוא הטוב שנא' אני אעביר כל טובי על פניך והוא הבית שנא' עליו בכל ביתי נאמן הוא כי טוב האדם ביתו · ועל כן אמר על עצמו אנכי האל בית אל · וכן ביעקב ויקרא למקו' אל בית אל והנה הכתוב הזה נכון כפשוטו כי המלאך הזה שהוא אל ביתאל והבן זה ·

† Shechinah, which means habitation, is feminine, and, therefore, the pronouns and verbs are feminine.

מלאך האלהים, where האלהים is by Gematria equivalent to מלאך; and אלהים (God) is here used, because she proceeds from the sphera, גבורה (might)."*

Here also it is plainly admitted that the angel calls himself the God of Bethel, and to this Being the vow was made. The fact therefore is not disputed, and therefore this one passage is sufficient to prove that this angel is very God. Indeed the commentators quoted do not deny the inference, for when they say that this Being was the Shechinah, or habitation, they employ the same language used in the New Testament, as for instance, "In Him dwelleth all the fulness of the Godhead bodily." (Coloss. ii. 9.) When the law of Moses sets before us a being who says of himself that He is the God of Bethel, and that He is the object of Jacob's worship, what else can we conclude but that He is very God, especially as the great object of this law, throughout, is to enforce the unity of God? But it is to be observed that this passage does not stand alone, there are other similar assertions, equally plain and strong. In the third chapter of Exodus, this same Being is said to have appeared to Moses in the bush, and then without any intimation of a change of person, the text says, "And when the Lord, יהוה, saw that he turned aside to see, God called unto him out of the midst of the bush, and said, Moses, Moses! And he said, Here am I. And he said, Draw not nigh hither: put off thy shoes from off thy feet, for the place whereon thou standest is holy ground. Moreover, he said, I am the God of thy fathers, the God of Abraham, the God of Isaac, and the God of Jacob. And Moses hid his face; for he was afraid to look upon God." (Exod. iii. 4—6.)

* המלאך הנזכר למעלה אמר לו אנכי האל בית אל · והרמז לשכינה הנקראת מלאך כי היא הנראית לאבות ואליה היה הנדר וע"כ אמר אשר נדרת לי שם נדר כמו שפי' למעלה · ונקראת מלאך יען היות הנהגת העולם הזה על פיה · והבן שקראה מלאך האלהים האלהים בגמטריא מ"לאך בעבור יניקתה מן הגבורה אמר אלהים · — Edit. Venice, 1523, fol. 45, col. 1. The folios are not numbered, but I have counted them, reckoning the title folio as fol. 1.

To a plain reader, abiding by the common rules of grámmar and the usage of all languages, it would appear, that the angel of the Lord here calls himself the God of Abraham, Isaac, and Jacob. But it has been said that this is a Trinitarian prejudice; let us see, then, how the Jews, who are supposed to be free from this prejudice, understood the passage:—

Aben Ezra expresses his opinion thus: "*And when the Lord saw.*"—"These are also the words of Moses, afterwards, and the angel is called by the glorious name in the same way as in the passage, 'For my name is in him,' and there I shall explain it. And this is also done with respect to the angel who appeared to Gideon, where it is written, 'And the LORD said to him.' Or the meaning may be thus, The Lord saw that he turned aside to see, and commanded the angel to call to him, and, therefore, the word אלהים (God) is used. [God called unto him out of the bush.] And this name [אלהים] is not a noun of substance, but a noun of quality, as I will explain: and it comprehends all holy beings, which are not corporeal, and whose power is not corporeal, as it is written, 'The Gods, אלהין, whose dwelling is not with flesh,' which is corporeal. And, behold, אלהים (God) in this passage, is the angel mentioned above."* (Comment. in loc.) Aben Ezra here offers two ways of interpreting the fourth verse; according to the first, there is no change of person. The angel is, therefore, the only agent throughout, and consequently says, "I am the God of Abraham, &c." According to the other interpretation there are two agents, Jehovah and the angel. The sense of the verse on this view would be, "When the Lord

* גם אלה דברי משה בסוף ונקרא המלאך בשם הנכבד כדרך כי שמי בקרבו ושם אפרשנו וכך המלאך שנראה לגדעון ושם כתוב ויאמר לו יי׳ או השם איננו שם העצם רק שם תאר כאשר אפרש והוא כולל כל קדוש שאינו גוף ולא כח בגוף ככתוב להן אלהין די מדרהון עם בשרא לא איתוהי שהוא הגוף והנה אלהים במקום הזה הוא המלאך הנזכר׃

saw that he turned aside to see, the angel called unto him out of the midst of the bush." We do not stop to show the untenableness of this interpretation at present, for it does not alter the argument. Aben Ezra grants that the angel is the speaker, and that is all that we require. We only wish at present to establish the fact, not to explain it.

R. Bechai testifies unreservedly to the fact, that the angel here calls himself the God of Abraham, Isaac, and Jacob. "Ask not," he says, "how Moses could hide his face before the angel, for the angel mentioned here is the angel, the Redeemer, of whom it is written, 'I am the God of Bethel.' And in like manner it is said here, 'I am the God of thy father, the God of Abraham, the God of Isaac, and the God of Jacob,' and he it is of whom it is said, 'My name is in him.'" (Comment. in loc.)

R. Moses ben Nachman goes a step farther; he not only confirms the fact, but rejects the explanation, that the angel was speaking in the name of him that sent him. His words are, "The explanation, that in the words, 'I am the God of thy father,' the messenger spoke in the language of him that sent him is not correct, for Moses's degree in prophecy was too high for him to hide his face before the angel. Our rabbies have said in Bereshith Rabba, 'This angel is Michael. As in the case of R. Jose, the Patient, wherever he was seen, they said, There is our holy rabbi; so wherever Michael is seen, there is the glory of the Shechinah.' They meant to say, that at first Michael appeared to him, and that the glory of the Shechinah was there, but he did not see the glory, for he did not apply his mind to the prophetic vision; but, when he applied his mind and turned aside to see, then the appearance of the Shechinah was revealed

* ואל תתמה איך יסתיר משה פניו מן המלאך כי המלאך הנזכר בכאן הוא המלאך הגואל שכתוב בו אנכי האל בית אל וכן אמר בכאן אנכי אלהי אביך אלהי אברהם אלהי יצחק ואלהי יעקב והוא שנ׳ עליו כי שמי בקרבו :

unto him, and God called unto him out of the midst of the bush. And in the way of truth, this angel was the angel, the Redeemer, for it is said, 'My name is in him.' He it is who said to Jacob, 'I am the God of Bethel;' and of him it is said, 'And God called to him.' But he is called angel, מלאך, with reference to the government of the world; and thus it is written [in one place], 'And the LORD brought us out of Egypt' (Deut. vi. 21); and [in another place] it is written, 'And he sent an angel, and hath brought us forth out of Egypt.' (Numb. xx. 16.) Again, it is said, 'The angel of his presence saved them,' that is to say, The angel who is his presence. (Isaiah lxiii. 9.) For it is written, 'My presence shall go, and I will give thee rest.' (Exod. xxxiii. 14.) And this is what is said, 'The Lord whom ye seek shall suddenly come to his temple, even the messenger of the covenant whom ye delight in: behold, he shall come. (Mal. iii. 1.)' And thou wilt understand this further in other verses yet to come, which treat of the same matter."

We have here the confession of Jews, that that Being who is called the angel of the Lord says of himself, that he is the God of Abraham, Isaac, and Jacob; that this is the plain meaning of the text, what, then, is the conclusion? What can it be, but that He is what he claimed to be? We have seen that there is but one being who is called the angel of the Lord. Secondly, That the name of this one Being is Jehovah, the incommunicable name of God: and, Thirdly, That this Being says of himself, distinctly and unequivocally, that He is the God whom Jacob worshipped, the God of Abraham, Isaac, and Jacob; and we have seen, Fourthly, That this is as plainly asserted by the Jews as by us. There is but one possible conclusion, and that is, that this Being is very God.

Enough, I trust, has been here said, to establish the

fact: it would take a volume to go through all the passages of the Bible, and more than one volume, to collate the passages of the rabbies. Schöttgen has given many more from more ancient books, but I have quoted commentators, who were almost cotemporary with Kimchi, to show what was the Jewish opinion of his time.

CHAPTER II.

(In the English Bible, chap. i. 18.)

1. (i. 18.) "*Then I lifted up.*"—In this vision he turned to behold another vision, clearer than the first, for he understood from it, that the horns were to push with, as (Deut. xxxiii. 17), "His horns are like the horns of an unicorn; with them he shall push the people together," but he did not understand who these horns were.

"*Four horns.*"—These are the four monarchies, and they are the Babylonian monarchy, the Persian monarchy, and the Grecian monarchy;* and so the Targum of Jonathan has it, "the four monarchies." And these four did evil unto Israel, as the angel exclaims, saying, "which scattered Judah, Israel, and Jerusalem."

2. (i. 19.) "*And I said ——— which scattered.*"—They pushed them even until they scattered them hither and thither; each of the horns in its time did them evil. For the Persian monarchy, although at its beginning it brought them up from their captivity, afterwards did them evil, in the days of Artaxerxes the First, and in the days of Ahasuerus until the second year of Darius.

3. (i. 20.) "*And the Lord showed me four workmen,*" as in Isaiah xliv. 13, "The workmen of wood,"† in order to cut off the horns, that is to say, each kingdom shall be a carpenter, to cut off the kingdom that preceded it, for the Babylonian monarchy fell by the hand of the Persian, and the Persian monarchy fell by the hand of the Greek. Or the carpenters may signify in a parable,

* He does not mention the fourth.

† The English has in both places carpenter, as Kimchi explains. I have translated literally "workmen," in order to show how our translators had the best authority for this choice of words.

the kings,* the supernal princes, who are appointed over the kingdoms; and our rabbies of blessed memory have interpreted the verse of the days of the Messiah, saying, "Who are the four carpenters? R. Simeon Chasida says, They are Messiah, the Son of David; and Messiah, the son of Joseph, and Elias, and the righteous priest. (Cohen Tsedek.)" †

"*And he spake* ——— *so that no man did lift up up his head.*"—They pushed and scattered them in such a manner, that no man of the children of Israel did lift up his head, because of them. כְּפִי signifies "so that," "in such a manner that;" according as in Exod. xii. 4, "Every man, כפי, according to his eating:" and so Jonathan has translated it, "And they did not permit any man to walk with an upright stature." לְיַדּוֹת signifies "to cast out," as in Lam. iii. 52,‡ וַיַּדּוּ, "They cast a stone upon me."

5. (ii. 1.) "*And I lifted up.*"—In this vision he turns to behold another vision. And it is certain that this vision is of the future, referring to the days of the Messiah, as the visions of Ezekiel, in which he saw the angel measuring Jerusalem in its length and breadth.

* Buxtorf reads מלכים, kings, but the whole phraseology here employed, shows that Kimchi alluded to the מלאכים, angels, whom the Jews suppose to be appointed over the nations of the earth, as may be seen in Rashi's Comment. in Isaiah xxiv. 4, Dan. x. 20, &c. The legend itself is thus given in the Pirke Eleazar—"The Holy One, blessed be He, descended with the seventy angels who surround the throne of his glory, and confounded their language into seventy nations and seventy languages, each nation with its own writing and language, and over each nation he appointed an angel, but Israel fell to his portion and lot, and, therefore, it is said, 'The Lord's portion is his people.'" (Deut. xxxii. 9.) Chap. xxiv. Edit. Sabionet. fol. 17, col. 1.

† This passage is found in the Talmud. Succah, fol. 52, col. 2, where Rashi says, in his Commentary, on the authority of the Bereshith Rabba, that "The righteous priest" means Shem, the son of Noah, who is there supposed to be identical with Melchisedek.

‡ English, 53.

"*A measuring line.*"—A line with which they measure. And this man was another angel, who did not speak with him.

6. (English 2.) "*To measure,*" לָמֹד, is the Infinitive, from מדד, the same form as לָרֹס אֶת-הַסֹּלֶת ("to sprinkle the fine flour," Ezek. xlvi. 14), from רסס; and, again, רַב לָכֶם סֹב ("It is enough for you to compass,"* Deut. ii. 3), from סבב.

7, 8. (English, 3, 4.) "*And behold ——— and he said unto him, Run, speak to this young man.*" But he himself did not speak to him (Zechariah); because this other angel had spoken with him from the beginning, He said to him, that he should speak thus, although he (Zechariah) saw the angel measuring the length of Jerusalem, and its breadth.†

"*Jerusalem shall be inhabited as towns without walls,*" i. e., Many shall live without the city, for the city will not contain them. Although the city shall be much longer and broader than it was, many shall live outside. פְּרָזוֹת signifies cities,‡ without a wall, or gates, or bars, for they shall dwell securely, so as to be afraid of no man, for I will be unto it a wall of fire.

"*This young man.*"—It may be, that he was a young man in years when he prophesied, as Samuel and Jeremiah: or he was the servant of another prophet greater than himself, and is, therefore, called "a young man," as in the case of Joshua; "His servant Joshua, the son of Nun, a young man." (Exod. xxxiii. 11.)

9. (English 5.) "*For I —— will be a wall of fire,*" so that no man will touch them to do them evil, as no man would touch fire, lest it should burn him.

"*The glory in the midst of her.*"—The object of the

* I translate literally, to show the Infinitive form.

† And might, therefore, have inferred it himself.

‡ One cannot help thinking of the cities of England, to which God has so long given this blessing.

glory is to protect them, as it is written in the prophecy of Isaiah, iv. 5, " And the Lord will create upon every dwelling-place of Mount Zion, &c."

10. (English 6.) " *Ho, ho*," is the language of calling, and is doubled for the sake of strength. And thus in the 11th (7th) verse, " Ho, deliver thyself, O Zion."

" *And flee from the land of the north*."—This is said in reference to those who remained in Babylon, who did not come up at the first, that they should make haste to go forth, and to return, and build the House (the Temple), for the time is come. The Vau in וְנֻסוּ is to be taken as in Psalm lxxvi. 7 (6), נִרְדָּם וְרֶכֶב וָסוּס, (" Both the chariot and horse are cast into a dead sleep"), and it shows that a word is left out, that is to say, their meaning is, " Come forth, and flee." *

" *For as the four winds of heaven*"—that is, when I said, that they should go forth from their captivity, I intended only those who were led captive to Babylon, as it is written, " Thou that dwellest with the daughter of Babylon ;" for the others are far away from them, for I have spread them abroad in captivity as the four winds, which are widely separated the one from the other ; thus, as to the four corners of the world, the east is far from the west, and the north from the south, so Israel is far one from the other in their captivity, and their time is not yet come to go forth, except for the captivity of Judah, therefore it is said, ' Ho, Zion, deliver thyself ; ' by which is meant the tribes of Judah and Benjamin, for they dwelt in Zion. Our rabbies, of blessed memory, have given a mystical interpretation to the words, ' As the four winds ; ' that, as the world cannot exist without the four winds, so neither can it exist without Israel." †

12. (English, 8.) " *For thus saith the Lord —— after*

* And so our translators have rendered it. This is another proof of the diligence of our translators in consulting the best authorities.

† Talmud Bab. Taanith, fol. 3, col. 2.

the glory hath he sent me."—After the glory which he promised you, as it is written in the prophecy above, the end of which is, "I will be a glory in the midst of her." After this he hath sent me unto the nations which spoiled you, for God, blessed be He, does not think it a sufficient blessing to repay you for the evil change which came upon you in the captivity, until he have taken vengeance upon your enemies, who spoiled you.

"*For he that toucheth you.*"—He that toucheth you shall not go unpunished, as a man who touches the apple of his eye, i. e., the pupil of the eye, which he will force out, if he touch it violently, so he that toucheth you for evil, toucheth himself.

13. (English, 9.) "*For, behold I ——— and they shall be a spoil to their servants,*" that is to say, the nations shall be a spoil to Israel, who were their servants during the captivity.

"*And ye shall know.*"—At that time, when this prophecy draws near, ye shall know that the Lord of Hosts hath sent me, and this will be in the time to come, in the days of the Messiah.

14. (English 10.) "*Sing and rejoice.*"—It is right to interpret this prophecy as far as "his holy habitation," of the future, in the days of the Messiah, because it is said, "Many nations shall be joined to the Lord," i. e., all flesh, and this we did not see during the second temple. But the subject of the rest of the parashah refers to the time of the second temple, for it speaks of Joshua and Zerubbabel.

"*Shall be joined.*" — This is plain; נִלְווּ signifies joining.

16. (English, 12.) "*Inherit — Judah,*" for he is the portion of God, blessed be He. Then he shall inherit him, for his inheritance will be in the Holy Land, for he shall have gone forth from the captivity, and shall be the inheritance of the blessed God in the Holy Land.

This verse is similar to "The Lord's portion is his people, Jacob the lot of his inheritance." Judah is mentioned, because he is the head of the kingdoms of Israel, and if it alludes to the second temple, Judah was he who had returned from captivity.

17. (English, 13.) הַס means "Be silent;" as we have explained.

"*For he is awaked up out of his holy habitation,*" that is, heaven.—He says, "Is awaked up," in the way of a parable, as a man who is awaked up from his sleep, in the same way as it is said, "Then the Lord awaked as one out of sleep." (Psalm lxxviii. 65.) נֵעוֹר is the Niphal conjugation of the verbs Ain Vau,* after the fashion of נָכוֹן, נָבוֹן, although they have got a kametz under the Nun, and this has got a tsere.

* Lit. Quiescents in the Ain.

CHAPTER III.

1. "*And he showed me,*" *&c.*—Satan is spoken figuratively of Sanballat and his companions, who were adversaries to them, and caused them to stop from their work. Jonathan has thus interpreted it, "And the sinner * stood at his right hand to oppose him.

2. "*And the* LORD, יהוה, *said.*"—This is said of the angel, who is called by the name of his master, and so, in the history of Gideon, and other places. †

"*The Lord rebuke thee.*"—This refers to God, blessed be He.

"*That hath chosen Jerusalem,*" to build it, and thou canst not resist him.

"*Is not this a brand plucked from the fire?*"—As a burning brand which is removed from the fire, that it may not burn any more, so was this man (Joshua) delivered from the fire of captivity to come to Jerusalem, and to build the house, and to minister therein. And our rabbies of blessed memory, have interpreted it of him, according to the literal sense, that he was along with Zedekiah and Ahab, when the king of Babylon burned them in the fire, and they were burnt, but he was delivered, ‡ as is said in that D'rash, § and so Jonathan has interpreted. ||

3. "*Now Joshua was clothed with filthy garments.*"—This is explained parabolically of his sons, who married strange women, and so is the interpretation of Jonathan,

* Buxtorf says, "By Synechdoche for Satan, because he sins, and makes others to sin."—Lex. Talm.

† This is another most important admission, and, at the same time, a precaution against the idea of a plurality, here so plainly intimated.

‡ See Talm. Bab. Sanhedrin, fol. 93, col. 1.

§ Drash, signifies a mystical interpretation.

|| Jonathan says nothing of this fable.

"Joshua had sons who had married women, not lawful for the priesthood." And so our rabbies of blessed memory have said, "That on account of this sin, that his sons married women unsuitable for the priesthood, and that he did not restrain them, therefore it is said, 'Joshua was clothed with filthy garments;' not* that it was Joshua's way to wear filthy garments, but that his sons took women unsuitable for the priesthood, and he did not restrain them." And so it is written in Ezra, "And among the sons of the priests there were found that had taken strange wives, namely, of the sons of Jeshua, the son of Jozadak, and his brethren." (Ezra x. 18.)

"*And he answered*,"† i. e. the angel. He said to the other angels who were standing before him, for he was greater than they, and he it was who sent them. And the Targum of Jonathan has, "To those who served before him."

"*Take away.*"—A type, that they should separate from the strange wives.

"*Thine iniquity.*"—The filthy garments represented the iniquity.

מַחֲלָצוֹת signifies changes of pure raiment, and this also represents, in a parable, the merits (of his good actions), that is to say, when the iniquity is put away, thy merits will appear. And Jonathan has interpreted thus, "I will clothe thee with merits."

5. "*And I said.*"—The prophet Zechariah says, I said to the angel that they should set a fair mitre upon his head. As thou hast commanded to take away the filthy garments from off him, and to clothe him with change of raiment, command also, that they should put a fair mitre on his head, that he may be consecrated as high-priest, for the mitre was worn on his head.‡

* The negative appears to be omitted in the Hebrew.

† Kimchi has, "And the angel answered."

‡ i. e., The mitre was peculiar to the high-priest.

"*And clothed him with garments*" (must be taken to mean) And they had *already* clothed him with garments; for before any mention is made of Zechariah, it was already said, "And I will clothe thee with change of raiment." (Ver. 4.) And thus (the Vau, "and," has a similar force) in Exod. xvi. 20, וַיָּרֻם תּוֹלָעִים וַיִּבְאַשׁ, "And it bred worms, and it stank;" i. e., for it already stank, for every thing stinks before it breeds worms. And again in Isaiah lxiv. 4, (5) הֶן־אַתָּה קָצַפְתָּ וַנֶּחֱטָא, "Behold, thou art wroth; *for* we have sinned," † and other like passages.

"*And the angel of the Lord stood by.*"—According as he saw in the prophetic vision, for until they had set the pure mitre upon his head, the angel of the Lord stood, so as not to move from his sight.

6. "*And the angel of the Lord protested.*"—He protested to him concerning this thing. And thus [we find the word used] in Deut. viii. 19, "I protest unto you, that ye shall surely perish;" and again, Gen. xliii. 3, "The man did solemnly protest unto us." The letter ע is pointed with pathach, because it is a guttural. According to the rule, it ought to have had a segol (וַיָּעֶד), as וַיָּשֶׁב אֵת כָּל־הָרְכֻשׁ, "And he brought back all the goods." (Gen. xiv. 16.)‡

7. "*Thus saith the Lord —— Thou shalt judge my house.*"—Inasmuch as he was High-Priest, and the other priests were to act by his command. "And I will give thee" (וְנָתַתִּי), expresses the future, and the Vau is used as in Exod. xix. 16, וַיְהִי בַיּוֹם הַשְּׁלִישִׁי, "And it came to

° Compare Noldius and Gesenius in ו.

† In Hebrew, "We have sinned," but our translators knew this signification of the ו, and translated as Kimchi here proposes. Here, in Zechariah, they have not done so, for it does not appear from the text that Joshua had been already clothed. The angel had given the command, but there is nothing to compel our belief that the command had been already executed.

‡ Consult Gesen. Lehrgeb.

pass on the third day;" and in Gen. xxii. 4, וַיִּשָּׂא אַבְרָהָם אֶת־עֵינָיו, "And Abraham lifted up his eyes." *

"*Places to walk among those that stand by.*"—They were the angels who stand and endure for ever; and this means, thou shalt walk amongst them, i. e., his soul, when it should be separated from his body. The Targum of Jonathan says, "In the resurrection of the dead I will revive thee," &c. †

8. "*Hear now, thou, —— and thy fellows.*"—The other priests.

"*For they are men of sign.*" ‡ They are worthy of having a sign wrought for them by their hands. And our rabbies of blessed memory have thus interpreted, "Who are men of sign or miracle? They are those for whom a miracle was wrought, i. e., Hannaniah, Mishael, and Azariah." §

"*For behold, I will bring my servant, the Branch.*"—This is Zerubbabel. || (Literally, "I am bringing.") The

* It is a Vau conversive.

† And give thee feet to walk among these seraphs.

‡ The marginal translation.

§ Talm. Bab. Sanhedrin, fol. 93, col. 1.

|| Kimchi here follows Rashi in interpreting "My servant, the Branch" of Zerubbabel. Their reason for this probably was, that if they acknowledged the person thus designated in this chapter to be the Messiah, they must have made the same admission in the parallel passage, chapter vi. 12; and by so doing, they would have admitted that Messiah was to be a priest as well as a king. Perhaps they also saw some polemical danger in this chapter, in connecting the promise of the Messiah, with the promise, occurring in the next verse, "To remove the iniquity of the land in one day," which would seem to favour the Christian doctrine, that the Messiah "by one offering, perfected for ever them that are sanctified." (Heb. x. 14.) But however that be, the interpretation which they propose is not tenable,

1st, Because it departs from the old received interpretation of the Jewish Church. Both Kimchi and Rashi admit that there was an interpretation referring this passage to the Messiah; and Jonathan, in his Targum, interprets both these passages of the Messiah.

2d, Because it contradicts the analogy of the prophetic language..

reason why it is said, "I am bringing" when he was already come, is, to signify that his dignity should increase still more, and his greatness should grow as a branch from the ground, which goes on growing; and thus it is said below (vi. 12), "Behold the man whose name is the Branch; and he shall grow up out of his place, and he shall build the temple of the Lord." And so Haggai, the prophet says, "I will take thee, O Zerubbabel," &c. (Haggai ii. 23.), as we have explained. But there are some who interpret "The Branch," of the Messiah, the King, and then the meaning is, Although I now give you this salvation, I will bring to you a greater salvation, in the time that I bring my servant the Branch. A mystical interpretation has also been given, whereby it appears that Menachem* (comforter) is the name of the Messiah; for Menachem is, by Gematria,† Tsemach

Messiah is elsewhere called "The Branch," as in Isaiah iv. 2, and Jeremiah xxiii. 6, in both which passages Kimchi himself freely admits that "Branch" means the Messiah.

3d, Because the words do not agree with the circumstances of Zerubbabel. God says, "I will bring my servant, the Branch." But, as Abarbanel remarks, Zerubbabel had come long before, and was already a prince among them. Kimchi felt this difficulty, and, therefore, tries to twist the words to mean, "that his dignity should increase still more, and his greatness should grow as a branch," &c. But Abarbanel remarks again, that God does not say that he will make him great, but that he will bring him; and adds, that "after this prophecy Zerubbabel attained to neither royalty, dominion, or other dignity, more than he already possessed." (See Abarbanel Comment. in loc.)

* Menachem (comforter) is said to be the name of Messiah in the Talm. Bab. Sanhedrin, fol. 98, col. 2, where the words, "The comforter (Menachem) that should relieve my soul, is far from me" (Lam. i. 16.), are cited in proof.

† Gematria is the same word as "geometry;" but in Jewish writings it designates a certain species of Cabbalistic interpretation, the principle of which is, that two words, whose letters amount to the same numerical value, signifying the same thing. Thus Menachem, consisting of מ=40, נ=50, ח=8, ם=40, amounts to 138. Tsemach, "branch," makes the same amount, for צ=90, מ=40, ח=8. A curious instance

(Branch.) Jonathan has also given this interpretation, "My servant, the Messiah."

9. "*For behold the stone,*" that is, the plummet, by which they make the building straight. Or, the meaning may be, The stone which they shall lay first, Zerubbabel shall lay it before Joshua, as it is said below (iv. 7), "He shall bring forth the head-stone."

"*Upon one stone seven eyes.*"—Upon every stone there shall be seven eyes, i. e., many watchings from God, blessed be He, on account of the enemies, who think to cause the work to cease. And these are the seven eyes of the Lord, spoken of below. (c. iv. 9.) "Seven" is a definite number to express a multitude, not literally seven, as in Levit. xxvi. 21, "I will bring seven times more plagues upon you, according to your sins;" and again, "The righteous falleth seven times and riseth again;" and such like. My Lord, my father, interpreted "seven" literally, to signify Joshua, Ezra, Zerubbabel, Nehemiah, and the three prophets, Haggai, Zechariah, and Malachi. Jonathan has interpreted, "Seven eyes looking to it."

"*Behold, I will engrave the graving thereof,*" or, "I will open the openings thereof." As if the stone had been bound up all the time that the work was stopped; and now he would loose it, and place it in the building. But the true meaning is "engraving," as in Exod. xxviii. 36, "And thou shalt grave upon it according to the graving of a signet." For as the finishing of the preparation of precious stone is the figures, and bloom and pomegranates, which they figure upon it by graving, so it is here said parabolically, i. e., I will finish it in all its preparation for the building.

of this occurs in the word נחש, serpent, which is made one of the names of Messiah, because its numerical value is = that of משיח (Messiah). Perhaps our Lord alluded to this interpretation when he said, "As Moses lifted up the serpent in the wilderness, even so shall the Son of Man be lifted up." (John iii.)

"*And I will remove.*"—וּמַשְׁתִּי is a transitive verb, but in Numb. xiv. 44, לֹא מָשׁוּ, "They departed not," is an intransitive. And this shall take place in the time in which the prophets promised an increase of Zerubbabel's dignity, as Haggai says, "I will take thee, Zerubbabel;" and Zechariah says, "I will bring my servant, the Branch." Then Israel shall be in prosperity in the time of the second temple, therefore it is said, "Ye shall call every man his neighbour."

"*The iniquity of the land*" may be taken literally, or, it may signify the punishment, as in Gen. xv. 16, "The iniquity of the Amorite is not yet full;" that is to say, that he would remove from them all evil and all affliction, and they should be in prosperity.

10. "*In that day ye shall call,*" on account of the abundance of peace which ye shall have.

CHAPTER IV.

1. "*And the angel came again and waked me.*"—In the other visions he says, "I lifted up mine eyes," because he saw of himself; but the angel waked him to see this vision.

יֵעוֹר מִשְּׁנָתוֹ ("*that is, wakened out of his sleep*"). This verb is in the Niphal conjugation, and is thus to be interpreted, "He waked me, and I was awakened as a man that is wakened out of sleep."

2. ויאמר. The k'thiv (the text) has the third person, "And he said," which is a continuation of the narrative; but the k'ri (the marginal note) has וָאֹמַר, the first person, "And I said," which refers to the words of Zechariah.

"*And her bowl,*" וְגֻלָּהּ. The point in the ה is mappik, and the word is not the third person feminine (of a verb). A similar instance is in Isa. xxviii. 4, כְּבִכּוּרָהּ בְּטֶרֶם קַיִץ, ("As *her* hasty fruit before the summer.") And again, Job xxviii. 11, וְתַעֲלֻמָה יֹצִא אוֹר* ("And her secret bringeth he forth to light.") And again, Ezek. xxii. 24, גֻשְׁמָהּ בְּיוֹם זָעַם, ("And her visitation with rain [did not take place] in the day of indignation.")

"*And his seven lamps thereon;*" like the candlestick in the law. And the middle one is a type of the Deity, who forms the bond of union to unite contraries. And thus the seven doubles † are contraries, and the governors

* Kimchi appears to have read with a Mappik.

† By the seven doubles, Kimchi means the letters in which a dagesh can occur. We now commonly reckon only six, בגד כפת, but the rabbies include the ר, as some instances are found where it is doubled. (See Gesen. Lehrgeb., § 37, 1.) In this reduplication the Cabbalistic writers find great mysteries, to which Kimchi here alludes. For instance, Saadiah Gaon says, "As these letters have got two opposite states (the dageshed and the undageshed), by their means were established those things which have got opposites. By means of the

to the world, which is made up of contraries, are the seven planets;* and the world has also six sides and three planes (dimensions), but the master of the sides is the seventh, and that is the centre; and thus it is with the body of every thing. But the author of the book of Jetzirah attributes to the world six sides, answering to the six points, and the holy temple situate in the middle.† He mentions the thing most honoured among all creatures.

"*Thereon,*" i. e., on the candlestick; and the bowl was above them; and he showed him this vision to inform him, that God, blessed be He, gives light to Israel, which is the contrary of their having been in darkness.

"*Seven and seven pipes to the lamps.*" ‡—The whole had seven pipes; one pipe to each lamp. And Rashi, of

dageshed letters, were created the things that are strong, as life, peace, riches, seed, grace, dominion, wisdom; and by means of the undageshed letters, were created the opposites of these. (Comment. in Sepher Jetzirah, edit. Mantua, fol. 88, col. 1.)

* According to the Jewish astronomers, the seven planets are, the Sun, Venus, Mercury, the Moon, Saturn, Jupiter, Mars, which were, according to Saadiah, in the place just cited, created by means of the seven double letters, and have, therefore, a double power of good and evil, according to their position with respect to the signs of the Zodiac. The rabbies believe in astrology, as may be seen abundantly in the commentaries to this book of Jetzirah, and in Aben Ezra's Commentary on the Tenth Commandment, &c. &c. They also believe that the heavenly bodies and spheres are living and intelligent beings, to whom is committed the management of things here below, as may be seen in Maimonides. (Hilchoth Jesode Torah, c. iii., and Moreh Nevuchim, part ii. c. 5.)

† The passage to which Kimchi alludes is as follows, "The seven double letters, בגד כפרת, answer to the seven extreme points. Of these six are, the zenith and the nadir, the east and the west, the north and the south, and the holy temple is placed in the centre, and it bears them all." The Commentary on which passage tells us, that "the holy temple is a mystical expression to signify the Creator." (Sepher Jetzirah, edit. Mantua, fol. 77, col. 1. Compare also fol. 103, col. 1.)

‡ Seven several pipes. (Marginal Translation.)

blessed memory, has explained that there were seven pipes to each lamp.

"*Pipes*," מוּצָקוֹת, pourers; an adjective instead of a verb,* and this name was used, because they were pouring oil from lamp to lamp.

3. *And two olive-trees*."—And again I saw two olive-trees, either on the candlestick or on the bowl, but this is much the same.

"*One upon the right of the bowl, and the other upon the left thereof*." (עַל-שְׂמֹאלָהּ.)—The same as משמאלה, i. e., על has the same force as מ. But he says, they were upon the bowl, and in a following verse (11) he says, "Upon the right of the candlestick, and on the left thereof;" the sense, however, is the same.

4. "*So I answered*," is clear.

5. "*And the angel answered*," is clear.

6. "*Then he answered — Not by might, nor by power*." —As thou hast seen the work of the candlestick, that it was done of itself, and without any man or thing arranging the lamps, or pouring oil into them, thus shall the building of the temple be effected without the power of man, solely by the Spirit of God, blessed be He, and by his good pleasure. But he afterwards explains to him the vision in detail.

7. "*Who art thou, O great mountain*."—He says, in reference to Sanballat and his companions who were opposing, Though thou be like a great mountain, before Zerubbabel thou shalt become a plain, and shall not be able to stand before him to stop the work.

"*And he shall bring forth the head-stone*."† As he brought forth the head-stone, when he began the building, in the twenty-fourth day of the ninth month, so he shall finish the work.

* The Michlal Jophi reads פועל, "the active participle." Kimchi makes the root יצק: Gesenius says, צוק.

† Kimchi takes והוציא in the past time.

"*With shoutings, Grace, grace.*" When Zerubbabel laid the head-stone in the building, he laid it with shoutings and a great tumult, and all the people said, Grace, grace, to this stone from God, blessed be He. The repetition of the word is to increase the force, as "Peace, peace, to him that is far off." (Isaiah lvii. 19.)

8, 9. "*Moreover the word of the Lord came.—— The hands of Zerubbabel shall make an end of it,*" i. e., shall finish it. And thus the verb בצע is used in Isaiah x. 12, "Wherefore it shall come to pass, when the Lord hath performed his whole work upon mount Zion," i. e., finished.

10. "*For who hath despised the day of small things?*" For when they began to build, their enemies stopped the work, and, behold, that day was the day of small shoutings,* and they despised that day during all the years that the work was interrupted, but now, when they see the plummet in the hand of Zerubbabel, they will rejoice.

"*The plummet,*" i. e., "the stone," the tin perpendicular, which is in the hand of the builder, to make the building straight. The governing word to "tin," is left out; the complete form is הָאֶבֶן אֶבֶן הַבְּדִיל, "The stone, the stone of tin." The perpendicular weight was made of tin or lead, and is called a stone, as the weights are called stone in Deut. xxv. 13, "Thou shalt not have in thy bag a stone and a stone," i. e., divers weights.

"*These seven.*"—The same as he said above; "Upon one stone seven eyes." (iii. 9.) "*They are the eyes of the Lord, which run to and fro through all the earth,*" and he sees those who persecute Israel, and he will keep them from their hand, that they should not rule over them.

11. "*And I answered.*" †—He had understood the matter of the candlestick, for it had been exhibited to him to show him light and joy, and the angel had ex-

* Kimchi supplies shoutings; the Michlal Jophi has the same.

† Zechariah did not ask for an explanation of the candlestick.

plained to him concerning the candlestick, that it was made of itself, to show him, that it was not by might nor by power: and now he asked him about the signification of the two olive-trees, and the two branches of the olive-trees, and the two golden pipes; and though his question (about the latter) is not mentioned in the vision, we learn that he saw them. The angel replied to the two questions briefly and mystically, "These are the two sons of oil;" and the prophet understood his answer.

12. "*And I answered — the two olive-branches.*"— From these two olive-trees proceeded two olive-branches, which were pressed "in the hand, ביד, of the two golden pipes," and they were pressed* of themselves. The meaning of "in the hand" is, In the midst (through, as in English); and behold, the olive-trees were pressed in the midst of the golden pipes, and the oil fell from the pipes into the bowl; and from the bowl it went forth to the tubes; and from the tubes to the lamps. And he compares these branches (שִׁבֲּלֵי) to ears of wheat (שִׁבֳּלִים), because they were full of olive-berries, as the ears are full of grains of wheat.

"*Pipes,*" צַנְתְּרוֹת, are vessels of the cruse-species (צַפַּחַת). Jonathan has rendered this word by אִסְקְרִיטְוָן (phials); and so Onkelos has rendered כצפיחית (like wafers, Exod. xvi. 31) by the same word.†

"*Which empty the golden oil out of themselves.*"— Oil clear as gold: and similar to this is the verse in Jer. li. 7, "Babylon hath been a golden cup in the hand of the Lord," i. e., the wine was clear and pure.

14. "*And he said, These are the two sons of oil.*"—

* i. e., The oil pressed out of them.

† In Hebrew, צפחת signifies a cruse, and צפחית, which is only a different form of the same word, signifies "a cake, wafer." In Chaldee the one word, אסקריטון, signifies both, though sometimes a distinction is made by the insertion of ׳ after א. (See Buxtorf Lex. Talm. in radic. אסק.)

יִצְהָר is the same as שֶׁמֶן, oil, as in Deut. xxviii. 5, corn, wine, וְיִצְהָר, or oil." Therefore he called them olive-trees, and they are Zerubbabel and Joshua; and he calls them "sons of oil," because they were anointed with the oil of anointing, the one to the kingdom, and the other to the priesthood.

"*That stand by the Lord of the whole earth*," for they are appointed to do his pleasure.—Jonathan has interpreted thus, "These are the two sons of princes, who stand before the Lord of the whole earth." But as to the matter of the two olive-trees and the two olive-branches, no explanation is given of what they signified. And, behold, the olive-trees represent Zerubbabel and Joshua, and the two branches that proceed from them represent their deeds, for with their hands they began the building of the temple. The two golden pipes represent Ezra and Nehemiah, who came after them, and by the hands of these four, light and good went forth to Israel.

CHAPTER V.

1. "*Then I turned ——— a flying roll.*"—He saw in a vision, a roll flying through the air, and this is also Jonathan's interpretation, "a flying roll."

2. "*And he said ——— the length thereof twenty cubits, and the breadth ten cubits.*"—It is not clear to what time this prophecy applies, but it seems as if it were spoken of the prophet's own times; for we have seen in the book of Ezra, that they were then guilty of many transgressions. And this curse went forth against stealing and false swearing; for, although stealing is not so grave an offence as false and lying oaths, yet thereby men are led to swear falsely. As to the circumstance, that he saw the measure of the length and the measure of the breadth, the commentators have explained this to mean, that he saw it going forth from the porch of the temple, of which the length was twenty cubits, and the breadth ten cubits, according to the building which Solomon built: and although it was then desolate, yet this roll had gone forth thence, for it had been spread out there, according to the measure of the length and the breadth; and this is what is meant by the expressions, "that goeth forth," and "I will bring it forth."

3. "*Then said he ——— This is the curse,*" the malediction.

"*Over the face of the whole earth,*" the land of Israel. —Jonathan has interpreted, "This is the oath* which shall go forth." The subject of this roll is similar to that seen by Ezekiel, which was written within and without (Ezek. ii.), and so this roll was written on both sides, and the writing was on one side, "Every one that stealeth shall be cut off; and on the other side, "Every one that

* מומתא, from ימא, jurare.

sweareth shall be cut off." The meaning of כָּמוֹהָ, "according to it," is the same as in Genesis xliv. 18, כָּמוֹךָ כְּפַרְעֹה ("For thou art even as Pharaoh"); and again, 1 Kings xxii. 4, כָּמוֹנִי כָמוֹךָ ("I am as thou art"); that is to say, the roll was written with curse and malediction on this side as on that side, and on that side as on this side; the meaning of נִקָּה is, "Shall be cut off," as in Exodus xxxiv. 7, נַקֵּה לֹא יְנַקֶּה. (English translation, "That will by no means clear the guilty.") נִקָּה is the conjugation Niphal. Although I have borne with them long until now, from henceforth they shall receive their punishment, for their time is come, therefore this roll went forth. The prophet saw the roll, but he did not see the writing upon it as Ezekiel did, until the angel told him, for the power of prophecy was gradually exhausting, and, therefore, the visions of Zechariah are obscure, and in Haggai, Zechariah, and Malachi, prophecy ceased.

4. "*I will bring it forth.*"—This curse I have brought forth to punish, from this time forth, the secret thief and the swearer, and I will no longer bear with them.

"*And it shall remain,*" וְלָנֶה. The curse shall abide in the midst of his house, until it consume him, and the timbers of his house, and the stones thereof.

5. "*Then the angel ——— went forth.*"—It appears that, after showing him the vision of the flying roll, the angel was hidden from him, and afterwards he went forth and showed him the vision of the ephah.

"*That goeth forth.*"—Going forth from the house of the Lord, as the former. Or the meaning may be, Going forth from the land of Israel. The Targum of Jonathan has, "Who are these that are revealed?"

6. "*And he said, This is the ephah that goeth forth.*" —He showed him the captivity of the ten tribes, who had long since been led away captive, how that they were utterly lost in the captivity, and did not now go forth, when the captivity of Judah and Benjamin went forth.

He showed him an ephah, which is a measure, to signify that God had measured out to them measure for measure; for, according as they had done by continuing many days in their wickedness, from the day that the kingdom was divided until the day that they were led away captive; and as they had not had one out of all their kings, who turned them to good, but, on the contrary, they all walked in an evil way; according, I say, as they had continued long in evil, so they shall be many days in captivity: this is measure for measure, therefore the prophet saw an ephah, which is a measure.

" *He said moreover, This is their eye in all the earth.*" Again the angel interpreted to him, and said, " This is their eye; " that is to say, this ephah, which thou seest, teaches, that there is an eye upon them, which sees their deeds, and which also sees in all the earth; as he said above, The eyes of the Lord that run to and fro through all the earth.

" *Their eye.*"—The eye that seeth them, i. e., the eye of the Lord.

7. " *And, behold, a talent of lead lifted up.*"—Was lifted up.

" *In the midst of the ephah.*"—כִּכַּר, talent, is feminine, as וְכִכַּר לֶחֶם אַחַת, " One loaf of bread " (Ex. xxix. 23); עֶשֶׂר כִּכְּרֵי־כֶסֶף, " Ten talents of silver." (2 Kings v. 5.) And a talent of lead is to teach us, that it was to make it heavy, and to sink it in captivity.

" *And this is one woman sitting in the midst of the ephah.*"—To whom does this woman refer? She is the ten tribes, who were included in one kingdom, and walked one way to evil, therefore, he calls her " one woman; " and she is sitting in the midst of the ephah, for she receives the measure which she meted withal.

8. " *And he said, This is the wickedness.*"—The angel said to the prophet, this ephah is the wickedness that was

in Israel, and that is, the ten tribes who made the calves, and began the service of Baal.

"*And he cast her into the midst of the ephah.*"—Therefore God, blessed be He, cast her into the midst of the ephah, for he measured to her according to her measure.

And he cast the weight of lead upon the mouth thereof."—To sink her in captivity many days. "The mouth thereof," means the mouth of the ephah. רִשְׁעָה may be a substantive or an adjective.

9. "*Then I lifted up mine eyes —— and beheld two women.*"—As we interpreted "one woman" to mean the ten tribes, so we will interpret the two women of Judah and Benjamin, who had been carried captive to Babylon. Although they had long since gone up from the captivity, when this vision happened, he showed him the vision for the sake of those who remained in Babylon, who were lazy to go up to Jerusalem, even after the building of the house had begun. And he said that he saw these two women going forth in captivity.

"*And the wind in their wings,*" i. e., They were very quickly carried captive to Babylon.

"*For they had wings like the wings of a stork,*" that is to say, wings long and broad like the stork's.

"*And they lifted up the ephah.*"—They lifted it up upon their wings, to show them that their captivity was in equity and in measure, as God measured to them for their evil deeds. The words, "between earth and heaven," are very plain; for he that flies, flies between the earth and the heavens, in the firmament of the heavens; and show that these two are not like the first woman, for upon her he cast a talent of lead to sink her in the earth, in the place of her captivity. But of these he did not speak to sink them in the earth, but they are suspended in the air, until the time that they returned to their land after the seventy years. The reason why he saw Judah and Benjamin as a vision of two women, and the ten tribes as one woman, is, because the tribe of Judah was kept distinct on account of the kingdom; and the tribe of Benjamin was joined with them more than the other tribes, because their portion was like one, and they were both carried captive together, therefore he says, "Two women." That great wise man, the Ràv, our rabbi, Moses, the son of Maimon, may his memory be blessed, has interpreted the two women of angels, whom he saw in the likeness of women, as he had also seen them in the likeness of horses, because the power of prophecy was languid in his time.*

10. "*And I said — whither do these bear the ephah?*"—He did not ask this in the first vision (but now), because he saw them bearing it away quickly. And what is the meaning of this, that the woman bore away the ephah? It is to show, that they caused the blessed God to pay them according to their measure. And it is as if he said, "*They carry themselves away captive.*"

11. "*And he said, to build her an house in the land of Shinar.*"—The ה in לָהּ, is rapheh.† This is what Jeremiah sent to them, saying, "This captivity is long, build ye houses, and dwell in them." (Jer. xxix. 28.)

"*And it shall be established, and set there upon her own base.*"—Their habitation shall be established there, that is to say, they have built houses there, and established their habitation there; and it is said, "Set these upon her own base," that is to say, the base that she has made for herself, because by the building of houses and planting of vineyards, they are lazy to go up from Babylon, who have remained there after that Ezra went up, and they did not wish to go up even after the building

* In the Moreh Nevuchim, part i., chap. 49.

† It might have a mappik. (See Michlal Jophi.)

of the house was begun. וְהֻנִּיחָה is a compound form from הניחה the Hiphil, and הונחה, the Hophal. And the reason of the composition is, that at first, when she was carried into captivity, הונחה, she was placed there without her will, and afterwards, הניחה, she placed herself there, i. e., she tarried there according to her own will, and was lazy to go up to Jerusalem.

CHAPTER VI.

1. " *And I turned ——— four chariots going forth from the two mountains, and the mountains were mountains of brass.*"—Visions of the four monarchies, which he had seen twice. Again he turned, and saw them a third time more clearly than on the former occasions. And a chariot. מרכבה is a team of four horses,* to show the strength of each in its time, when it ruled in the world, and each of them did evil to Israel. And again he saw them, that they were going forth between the two mountains: and this teaches us, that their strength was as the strength of mountains. And the mountains were mountains of נחשת, and that is the cutting iron, that is called atsir † in profane tongues. There are similar expressions in the Bible, and one of them is, " Walking with slander, brass and iron." ‡ (Jer. vi. 28.) The meaning is, that it is stronger than stone, for it cuts and graves stone; and it was to represent the strength more forcibly, that he showed him that they were mountains of brass (or steel). And again, נחשת is mentioned, because it is a noun, derived from נחש, to try, as נִחַשְׁתִּי וַיְבָרְכֵנִי יְהוָה בִּגְלָלֶךָ, " I have learned by experience that the Lord hath blessed me for thy sake." (Gen. xxx. 27.) And by the hand of the four kingdoms Israel was proved and tried.

* The rabbies infer that מֶרְכָּבָה, signifies a team of four horses, or a four-horse chariot, because it is said in 1 Kings x. 29, " And a chariot came up, and went out of Egypt for six hundred shekels, and an horse for an hundred and fifty." The price of the chariot is here four times that of the horse.

† *Acero* is the Spanish for steel; Kimchi thinks that נחשת signifies not brass, but steel. In Buxtorf's Bible this word is written אצ״ר, but in the Michlal Jophi it stands thus, איר״ץ, which is more correct.

‡ On this passage of Jeremiah, Kimchi also says, that נחשת signifies steel, but he says, that it is a mixture of brass and iron.

2. "*In the first chariot.*"—A type of the Babylonian monarchy, as I have explained.

"*Black horses.*"—These are the same as the speckled horses above. This is a type of the Medo-Perisan monarchy, and he called them above "speckled," and here black, for they are two nations, although but one kingdom. Some interpreters say, that he showed their colour black, because the faces of Israel were made black in their monarchy, and this was in the days of Haman. Other interpreters say, that these colours agree with their custom of dying their clothes, and that one was accustomed to the speckled colour, and the other to black.

3. "*And in the third chariot white.*"—A type of the Grecian monarchy, but we do not know why he has designated them by white. R. Saadiah, of blessed memory, has written, that it is on account of the first king of Greece, Alexander, the Macedonian, who was a wise man and philosopher; and as wisdom is a thing that is white and fair, therefore he designated that monarchy by the appellation white.

"*And in the fourth chariot grisled and bay horses.*"—In this chariot he saw two colours, "grisled," ברדים, which is a colour that has white spots, after the likeness of hail, and they are in the midst of another colour. And the reason why he showed him this colour in reference to the Roman empire, is, because they think to triumph over the law of Moses, which is white as hail, but they mix it with many creeds, as the hail is mixed with the colour that was in them (the horses), whether black or any other colour.

"*Bay.*"—Jonathan has rendered this word by קְטְמָנִין, i. e., that the colour thereof was the colour of ashes. This chariot is a type of the Roman monarchy, which humbled the Grecian monarchy, and has dominion in the world. He saw therein two colours, because there is another kingdom with her, which rules in the world, and that is the kingdom of Ishmael; and so it is said, in the kingdom of Nebuchadnezzar, as Daniel has interpreted it, " The kingdom shall be divided." (Dan. ii. 14.)

4. " *Then I answered.*"—Inasmuch as he had already seen two visions relating to this one matter, and as, in the second of the four horses, more light had been given him than in the first, according as the angel explained it to him; therefore when he saw again the four chariots, he knew that it was exhibited to him in order to communicate something new, and therefore asked the angel, " What are these, my Lord?" i.e., For what new information are these come? I have already seen that the visions represent the four monarchies; if so, what are these? for what purpose do I see them?

" *And the angel answered —— These the four winds of heaven.*"—Winds רוּחוֹת here signifies the same as לְרוּחוֹת to the winds. [There are similar cases where the preposition לְ, to, is omitted,] as וַיָּבוֹא יְרוּשָׁלַם, " And he came Jerusalem," i. e., to Jerusalem. (1 Kings iii. 15.) And again: בֶּן שָׁאוּל, " the son of Saul," for לְבֶן שָׁאוּל " to the son of Saul" (2 Sam. iv. 2); and other similar cases. The meaning is, These four chariots go forth to the four winds of heaven; i. e., to give permission to the four monarchies to rule in the four winds, each in its time, that is to say, in the whole world, which has four corners.

5. " *From standing before the Lord of the whole earth,*" i. e., commissioned by God, who sent them, according as it is said, " And the sons of God came to present themselves before the Lord." (Job i. 6.)

6. " *Which are therein.*"—He does not mention the red horses, for the Babylonian monarchy had already passed away. The Medo-Persian monarchy went forth first to the land of the north, which is Babylon, to destroy it, but afterwards ruled over all the kingdoms of the earth. The white horses, which represent the Grecian monarchy,

went forth after them, when their kingdom was strong; for behold, Alexander the Macedonian, the first King of Greece, slew Darius in Babylon, and took the kingdom from him, and afterwards had dominion, he and his successors, over the whole earth.

"*And the grisled go forth toward the country of Teman*," which is the south country, for Rome is to the north, and Lulianus Cæsar, who reigned over Rome, began to wage war against the kingdom of Greece; and in the beginning of his wars, he went forth to the land of Egypt, which is to the south. At that time the Greeks *ruled* over all lands, but this Lulianus Cæsar prevailed against them, and caused the kingdom to pass away from the Greeks, and turned it to the Romans.

7. "*And the bay*" (strong).—These signify the Turkish empire, who strengthened themselves to seek a kingdom in any place that might offer: and therefore he does not define any wind of heaven for them. This is what is said, "And they sought to go, that they might walk to and fro through the earth."

"And he said," i.e., Permission was given them to walk to and fro, and to subdue lands.

8. "*Then cried he upon me*."—He cried upon me with a loud voice, and said to me, "Behold these that go toward the north country have quieted my spirit in the north country; i.e., These black horses which went forth to Babylon to destroy it have caused a quieting of my spirit by destroying it.

"*Have quieted my spirit*."—My wrath which I had against them, because they did evil to Israel, more than enough, as is said, "I was a little displeased, and they helped forward the affliction."

9, 10. "*And the word of the Lord* —— *take*," *&c.* לָקוֹחַ is the infinitive instead of the imperative, as הָלוֹךְ וְקָרָאתָ "Go and cry." (Jer. ii. 2.)

"Take of the captivity" of those that have come from

the captivity, i. e. Hildai, and Tobijah, and Jedaiah, and Josiah, who had brought silver and gold as a free-will offering for the building of the temple. The word of the Lord came to the prophet, and made this known to him, and said to him that he should take the silver and the gold and make crowns thereof.

"*Come thou the same day,*" i. e., In the day that thou comest thither, for he had not told him to go there on the day of the prophecy.

"*And go into the house of Josiah the son of Zephaniah,*" for the others were in his house; and this is what is said, "Which are come from Babylon," Josiah and the others above-mentioned.

11. "*Then take silver,*" *&c.*—Thou shalt take from them silver and gold which they have brought in their hands as a voluntary contribution.

"*And make crowns.*"—Thou shalt make thereof two crowns, and place one upon the head of Joshua, to distinguish him as high-priest: and this is similar to the pure mitre which they placed on his head in the prophecy as is said above. As to the other crown, it was not necessary to mention what was to be done with it, for it is clear that it was to be upon the head of Zerubbabel, for he was in the place of king, and no king without a crown. And perhaps before they placed the crown on his head he was called governor, as it is written, "Governor of Judah" (Hag. i. 1): but after that the crown had been placed on his head they called him king, for, although this is not written, the circumstances warrant this opinion.

"*And make*" וְעָשִׂיתָ.—According to Ben Naphthali,*

* R. Jacob ben Naphthali, a Babylonian rabbi, and R. Aaron bn Asher, a learned rabbi of Tiberias, both of the 11th century, collected various readings from the manuscripts then existing. See the Prolegomena to Walton's Polyglott, iv. 9, and Horne's Introduction, vol. ii., p. 37.

this word is Milra, the accent is under the ח, but according to Ben Asher it is Milel, and the accent is under the שׁ, and so we read.

"*And speak unto him —— Behold the man whose name is the Branch;*" i. e., Behold a man is with thee who shall be the head of Israel, and that is Zerubbabel, and he shall be called the Branch, for his advancement shall be like a branch of the ground, which grows up gradually. Thus his degree shall gradually mount, until it be very great, as Haggai prophesied concerning him: "In that day, saith the Lord of hosts, will I take thee, O Zerubbabel," &c. (Hag. ii. 23.)

"*He shall grow up from under him.*"—From his place,* i. e., the place where he is, that is Jerusalem, from whence his advancement is to come.

13. "*Even he shall build.*"—This is said twice for confirmation.

"*And he shall bear the glory.*"—He shall bear the glory and majesty of royalty.

"*Upon his throne.*"—As the king who sits upon his throne and rules the land.

"*And shall be a priest upon his throne,*"† that is, before his throne. The preposition עַל has the same force above, מהתיצב על אדון כל הארץ, "From standing before the Lord of the whole earth." And thus [the priest is described]. (1 Sam. ii. 35.) "And he shall walk before mine Anointed for ever;" for the priest was accustomed

* Here again our translators agree with Kimchi. Hengstenberg thinks that the right translation is "De subter se germinabit," which contains the explanation of צֶמַח. The great personage here promised will bear the name "branch" with good reason, for he will not descend from above in full glory, but like a plant that shoots forth from the earth, gradually rise from the humility of his beginning." (Christologie, part ii. page 74.)

† Kimchi would translate, "And there shall be a priest before the throne." But this is evidently false; על כסאו, just two or three words before, means "upon his throne."

to come before the king to instruct him and to speak with him. But the king was not in the habit of coming before the priest, except when he consulted by means of the Urim and Thummim, as it is written, "And he shall stand before Eleazar the priest, who shall ask counsel for him, after the judgment of Urim before the Lord."

"*And the counsel of peace shall be between them both,*" for one shall not envy the other, and they both shall agree like one man in what they do.

14. "*And the crowns shall be.*"—Each of the crowns shall be to them for a memorial in the temple of the Lord, as it is said in the law, "For a memorial before the Lord" (Exod. xxx. 16): that is to say, their free-will offering shall ascend before the Lord for good to them in this world and that to come. Some interpreters say "for a memorial" means, that they should be remembered in the mouths of the coming generations, for their names shall be written and engraved upon them.

"*To Helem.*"—He is Heldai, whom he mentioned above, and he had two names.

"*And to Hen.*"—This is Josiah whom he had mentioned. Our rabbies, of blessed memory, have interpreted "in the temple of the Lord" to mean, that the crowns were placed there after they had been put on the heads of Zerubbabel and Joshua, and so it is in the treatise Middoth: "And golden chains were fixed in the beams * of the porch, by means of which the young priests went up and saw the crowns which were in the windows; for it is said, And the crowns shall be to Helem, and to Tobijah, and to Jadaiah, and to Hen the son of Zephaniah, for a memorial in the temple of the Lord."

15. "*And they that are far off.*"—Some of the Gentiles of the land shall come from a far country to build in the

* Middoth, c. iii. 8. See Surenhusius, p. v. 362. In the Mishna lately published at Berlin, חקרה is translated "Decke" (covering, or roof).

temple of the Lord; that is to say, to bring voluntary contributions for the building of the temple. And perhaps this was fulfilled in the days of Herod in the great building which he built in the house of the sanctuary. Some interpreters say, "They that are far off" refers to Israel scattered in the captivity in distant lands.

"*And this shall come to pass if ye will diligently obey.*" All this that I promise you shall come to pass if ye will diligently obey the voice of the Lord your God.

OBSERVATIONS ON CHAPTER VI. 9—15.

This is one of the many passages in which Rashi, Aben Ezra, and Kimchi depart from the ancient interpretation, and offer a new one less favourable to Christianity. These three rabbies assert, as in the third chapter, that the "man whose name is the Branch" signifies Zerubbabel, and make this exposition the turning-point of the whole interpretation, grammatical and doctrinal. They have thus begun at the wrong end. The first consideration must be the grammatical meaning, and when that is fixed, then comes the application of the sense to the particular person intended; and this is the order in which I shall offer my observations on this passage.

I. There are certain portions of this passage of which Kimchi endeavours to establish a grammatical exposition favourable to his own doctrinal interpretation. The first of these is in verse 11, וְעָשִׂיתָ עֲטָרוֹת "And thou shalt make crowns;" which Kimchi thus interprets: "Thou shalt make thereof two crowns." The word עֲטָרוֹת "crowns" is confessedly the plural of עֲטָרָה, "a crown," and if we look merely to the number, it may signify a thousand crowns as well as two. Two is therefore an entirely arbitrary exposition, or rather a gratuitous addition to the text. The context does not require the number two, for the following words are וְשַׂמְתָּ בְּרֹאשׁ יְהוֹשֻׁעַ, "And thou shalt set upon the head of Joshua the high-priest." The עטרות (crowns), whatever their number, whether two or two hundred, were to be set upon the head of Joshua. There is not one word said about setting them on the head of Zerubbabel, or any other person. Abarbanel thinks that, because silver and gold are both mentioned, there were two crowns, one of silver and the other of gold; but this does not necessarily follow. These two materials might be employed, whether there was only one crown or many crowns. There is therefore nothing to warrant Kimchi's assertion that two crowns were to be made.

But besides the plural form, we must also inquire, how this word, עֲטָרוֹת, is elsewhere used in the plural. It occurs first and most frequently as the proper name of a city, as עֲטָרוֹת וְדִיבֹן וְיַעְזֵר, "Ataroth (crowns), and Dibon, and Jazer." (Numb. xxxii. 3.) And again: "It went down from Janohah, to עֲטָרוֹת Ataroth (crowns), and to Naharath, and came to Jericho, and went out at Jordan." (Josh. xvi. 7.) And again: "Bethlehem and the Netophathite, עַטְרוֹת בֵּית יוֹאָב, the crowns of the house of Joab." (1 Chron. ii. 54.) In these and other passages the plural form, עֲטָרוֹת, is taken in a singular sense to stand for the name of one city, and the frequency of its occurrence in this singular sense would lead to the supposition, that it signifies one crown consisting of several smaller crowns or diadems;* and this conclusion is fully confirmed by

* Hengstenberg Christologie, part ii., p. 71, who gives as an illustration, Rev. xix. 12, "And on his head were many crowns," which as he says, "cannot mean that Christ wore many separate and distinct crowns, but one crown composed of several;" to which we may add the well-known triple crown. Hengstenberg does not mention the occurrence of עֲטָרוֹת as a proper name, but I think it an important part of the argument.

the only passage where it occurs as a common substantive. "Behold my desire is, that the Almighty would answer me, and that mine adversary had written a book: surely I would take it upon my shoulder, and, אֶעֶנְדֶנּוּ עֲטָרוֹת לִי, bind it as a crown to me." (Job xxxi. 15.) Here this plural plainly signifies one crown, not many, and we are thus authorised in using it in the same sense in the passage before us. And if further confirmation be necessary, we have it in the 14th verse, where this plural noun is construed with a singular verb.* וְהָעֲטָרוֹת תִּהְיֶה "And the crowns, it shall be to Helem and Tobijah," &c. This of itself would not be decisive, but is yet an important confirmation when taken in connexion with the preceding reasons. Had the verb been plural, it would have served to balance the decisive passage from Job, but now it confirms the inference that this plural form is to be taken in the singular, and that therefore only one crown is intended; and this exactly agrees with the command in the context, to set what was made on the head of one person.

The next passage, of which Kimchi endeavours to modify the sense, is, וְהָיָה כֹהֵן עַל־כִּסְאוֹ, "And he shall be a priest upon his throne." He says that עַל has here the same force as in verse 5: מֵהִתְיַצֵּב עַל־אֲדוֹן כָּל־הָאָרֶץ, "From standing before the Lord of the whole earth." He would therefore translate the whole sentence, "And there shall be a priest before his throne," or, "And a priest shall be before his throne," by which translation he makes a new subject to the verb substantive, and thus finds out two persons for the two crowns of which he had spoken before. Now, in the first place, granting for a moment that this translation of עַל is correct, it will not afford a sense agreeing with the context. To what purpose should Zechariah tell Joshua that there should be a priest before the throne, when he himself was already the high-priest? This translation will introduce a third

* Hengstenberg Christologie, part ii., p. 73.

person, which is quite beside Kimchi's purpose. Then, again, if Joshua was not to sit upon a throne himself, and was not even the type of him that was to sit upon the throne, to what purpose was he crowned? Crowns and thrones generally go together. But, secondly, this translation of Kimchi is not warranted by the text; for, first, he translates "And he shall be a high-priest upon his throne:" other Jewish interpreters translate differently. Jonathan Rashi, who otherwise agrees with Kimchi, says, in his note upon the words, "And he shall sit," "That is the high-priest upon the throne of the priesthood." Aben Ezra says still more expressly, "The high-priest Joshua shall also sit upon his throne, and there shall be no jealousy between them on account of the two thrones." Abarbanel, who supposes the words to refer to the high-priest in the days of the Messiah, translates עַל in the same way; he says, "At that time, which is still future, the priest shall sit upon his throne." It cannot therefore be said, that our English translation is a mere Christian translation made to suit Christian doctrinal interpretations. It is the translation authorised by the most famous Jewish names, and one of these commentators, Abarbanel, had Kimchi's Commentary before him, but yet rejected this interpretation as untenable. Secondly, It is not enough to show that עַל, when construed with הִתְיַצֵּב, signifies "*before*." Not this verb, but another, וְהָיָה, occurs in this passage; and in order to establish his translation, it will be necessary to show that עַל, when construed with הָיָה, has this signification; for every one knows that the meaning of the Hebrew prepositions varies very much, according to the verbs with which they are construed. But, thirdly, The context fixes the meaning of עַל, the word occurs before in this very verse, where Kimchi himself allows that it means "upon." The whole sentence is,

וְיָשַׁב וּמָשַׁל עַל־כִּסְאוֹ וְהָיָה כֹהֵן עַל־כִּסְאוֹ׃

"And he shall sit and rule upon his throne, and be a priest upon his throne," where it would be very strange, indeed, that the same preposition, governing the very same word twice in the same short sentence, should have two different significations. Kimchi's new translation, therefore, is not correct.

Having thus disposed of the verbal exposition, we now come to the application of the whole to Zerubbabel. Kimchi says, that "The man whose name is the Branch," is Zerubbabel, and that he it was who was to grow up out of his place, build the temple of the Lord, and sit and rule upon his throne; in which application he has trod in the footsteps of Aben Ezra and Rashi. To show the untenableness of this exposition is not very difficult. It has been done already by a bigoted Jew thoroughly hostile to Christianity, and confessedly one of the most able of their rabbies, Abarbanel; and as it may be interesting to see his line of argument, it is here subjoined:—

"Rashi has written, that the words, 'Behold the man whose name is the Branch,' have, by some, been interpreted of the Messiah. He here means Jonathan, whose interpretation he did not receive; for he adds, that the building here spoken of refers altogether to the second temple; and in like manner the interpreters have interpreted this whole chapter of the second temple. But I wish that I could ask them, if this prophecy refers to the second temple and Zerubbabel, why it is said, The man whose name is the Branch, and he shall grow up from beneath him, מתחתיו? Surely, we know that every man grows up from beneath him, and that from being a child, he grows up to manhood, and even to old age and hoary hairs. Rashi, perceiving this objection, has interpreted this to mean, that he should be of the royal seed; but this is not correct, for the word מִתַּחְתָּיו, teaches nothing about the royal family. R. Aben Ezra has interpreted מתחתיו to mean "of his own accord," but this is not true, for Zerubbabel did not rise up of himself, but by the command of Cyrus. If he said this in allusion to the words of Haggai, 'The Lord stirred up the spirit of Zerubbabel, the son of Shealtiel ——, and they came and did work in the house of the Lord;' this would prove too much, for it is written in the same place, 'And the spirit of Joshua, the son of Josedech, the high-priest, and the spirit of all the remnant of the people' (Haggai i. 14); so that, according to this, they might all be called 'Branches,' and of all it might be said, 'They shall grow up out of their place.' Rabbi David Kimchi says, 'He shall grow up out of his place, which is Jerusalem, whence his advancement is to come.' But after his arrival in Jerusalem, we do not see that he attained any dignity at all; though even if he had, what great news would it have been to say, that in the place where he is, there his advancement shall come? Even if it were so, the words, 'He shall grow up from beneath him,' would still remain an objection against this opinion. But, at all events, I should ask them, if these words be spoken of Zerubbabel, why does the prophet add, 'He shall build the temple of the Lord, even he shall build the temple of the Lord?' why this repetition to express one single event? The commentators have got no answer but this, It is to confirm the matter. But if that be the case, it would be better to repeat the words three or four times, for then the confirmation would have been greater still. I should further ask them, how they can interpret of Zerubbabel those words, 'He shall bear the glory, and shall sit and rule upon his throne,' *for he never ruled in Jerusalem, and never sat upon the throne of the kingdom, but only occupied himself in building the temple, and afterwards returned to Babylon.*" (Abarbanel Comment. in loc.) Here, then, we have the reasons which led a learned antagonist utterly to reject, as untenable, the notion, that this prophecy of the man whose name is the Branch, can refer to Zerubbabel. The last reason assigned is decisive, and must compel every honest interpreter to seek for some other person as the subject of the prophecy.* The tradition of the ancient Jewish Church,† and the parallel passages in Isaiah iv. and Jeremiah xxiii., point out the Messiah as that person, and this opinion is fully confirmed by the contents of the prophecy.

The prophecy is twofold; there is, first, a prophetic or symbolic action, and then a verbal prophecy to explain it. The prophetic action consists in taking gold and silver from certain men, who had come from Babylon, making a crown of these metals, setting it upon the heads of the high-priest first, and then depositing the crown in the temple. That there are such things as symbolical prophecies, or prophetic actions, no one that believes the Bible can deny. Not to go elsewhere, they abound in this book. The vision of the four horns and the four carpenters is of this nature. Again, the man measuring Jerusalem, chapter ii. The putting off the filthy garments from Joshua, which is also followed by a verbal prophecy concerning the man whose name is the Branch, chap. iii. Again, the candlestick and the olive-trees, chapter iv. Again, the flying roll and the ephah, chapter v. Again, the four chariots, in the beginning of the chapter under consideration. In every chapter, without exception, from the first to the sixth, we have symbolical prophecies, and in no case do the things or persons employed as symbols,

* The misapplication of the prophecy to Zerubbabel has, however, one important use in the Jewish controversy. It shows how little good faith there is in the common objection, that our Lord was not called Immanuel, but Jesus, and that, therefore, Isaiah vii. 14 cannot refer to him. Rashi, Aben Ezra, and Kimchi, all apply, "The man whose name is the Branch," to Zerubbabel, though it is certain that Zerubbabel is never thus called in Scripture. They thereby teach us, that in similar prophecies it is sufficient, that the character and circumstances of the person should answer to the meaning of the name.

† See the notes on chapter iii.

represent themselves, at some future period of their history, but they are symbols of other things and persons. The uniform nature, therefore, of all the preceding visions, decides that the action here described is symbolical, and that it does not symbolise any thing referring to Joshua, but to some one else. The symbols selected point out, first, that that person is to be a high-priest. Secondly, as Joshua was engaged in the building of a temple, the person symbolised should also build a temple. Thirdly, that he is to be crowned, that is, also to be a king. And, Fourthly, that persons from a distance, symbolised by those who had come from Babylon, should acknowledge his royal dignity, as these men contributed the gold and silver to make the crown.

The verbal prophecy promises the same particulars. First, " he shall be a priest upon his throne." Secondly, " he shall build the temple of the Lord." Thirdly, " he shall bear the glory" (הוד, the majesty *), and shall sit and rule upon his throne. " And they that are far off shall come and build in the temple of the Lord." It is not necessary to point out the well-known passages which prove that these four particulars are all features in Messiah's character, and in that of no one else. It is also easy to identify these features in the character of Jesus of Nazareth. He is represented in the New Testament as a high-priest, as a King; and it is certain that the Gentiles, who were then afar off, have acknowledged his dignity. The only apparent difficulty is the building of the temple. Did he build a temple? The nature of all the preceding visions removes this. The symbols represented something else, not any thing identical. The temple here spoken of cannot, therefore, be a literal temple, but something else that is symbolised; it is his natural and mystical body. " Destroy this temple, and in three days I will raise it up." (John ii. 19.) " In whom ye also are builded

* Hengstenberg, Christologie, part ii. p. 77.

together for an habitation of God through the Spirit." (Eph. ii. 22.)

The above remarks are sufficient to vindicate the Christian interpretation, but there is one feature in the verbal prophecy, on which I wish to say a few words. Vitringa and others interpret the personal pronoun "his," in the words, "He shall sit and rule upon *his* throne, and shall be a priest upon *his* throne," as referring to God, meaning that the Messiah should rule and be a priest upon the throne of God. Hengstenberg objects to this interpretation, but assigns no solid reasons for his dissent. The whole context appears to me not only to warrant, but to require this interpretation. The prophecy begins with promising Messiah as a man. "Behold! a man. Branch is his name." It then states what he should do. "He shall build (it is said, not his own temple, but) the temple of the Lord; and he shall bear the glory, and shall sit and rule upon his throne, and be a priest upon his throne." Here the structure of the sentence appears to me to lead the mind naturally to Him whose is the temple. But the concluding words, "And the counsel of peace shall be between them both," seem to me absolutely to require it. Who are the "both," between whom the counsel of peace is to be? Hengstenberg and others answer, the kingly estate and the priesthood; but this seems harsh and contrary to fact. The counsel concerning peace is not between Christ's kingly and priestly office, but between the Deity and Jesus of Nazareth as Messiah. The words "between them both," naturally convey to the mind the idea of two personal agents, not two offices. The only two personal agents mentioned in the preceding words, are, "The man whose name is the Branch, and "The Lord." To them, therefore, we naturally refer the words. If the word King had occurred in the text, that is, if the prophet had written, "He shall be a king upon his throne, and a priest upon his throne," Hengstenberg's interpretation would have had some colour, but the absence of this, along with the other reasons, serves to confirm Vitringa's opinion. This interpretation also agrees with the parallel passages in Isaiah and Jeremiah, where both the natures of Messiah are distinctly mentioned. In Isaiah iv. 2, "The branch of the Lord" is the divine nature. "The fruit of the earth," the human nature. In Jer. xxiii. 5, "I will raise up unto David a righteous Branch," is the human nature. "And this is the name whereby he shall be called, THE LORD our righteousness," is the divine nature. And so the prophecy under consideration concludes with a declaration that would naturally lead Zechariah to conclude, that the Lord himself should be the person here promised. The Lord who had been speaking to Zechariah all the way through says to him, "And ye shall know that the Lord of Hosts hath sent me unto you."

CHAPTER VII.

1, 2. "*And it came to pass* ——— *when they had sent*" וַיְהִי - וַיִּשְׁלַח (literally, "and it came to pass —— *and he* sent"). The meaning is, after they had sent.* [The conjunction ו has frequently this signification] as in Isaiah lxiv. 4 (5) :—הֵן אַתָּה קָצַפְתָּ וַנֶּחֱטָא, "Behold thou wast angry when we sinned"† [according to Kimchi]. And again, Lev. ix. 22, וַיֵּרֶד מֵעֲשֹׂת הַחַטָּאת, "*When*‡ he descended from offering the sin-offering," and other like. The sense is, After he had sent, the word of the Lord came to Zechariah. It is not said who sent. Some interpreters say that ביתאל (Bethel), "the house of the Lord," is the name of a man, and that he sent Sherezer and Regemmelech and his men from the captivity to Jerusalem. But the correct interpretation is, that ביתאל is to be taken literally of the house of the Lord. Jonathan has, "And he sent to Bethel." The senders were the children of the captivity, and though the singular number "He sent" is used, it is to be taken collectively; as in the third verse, "Shall I weep —— as I have done." The messengers were Sherezer and Regemmelech and his men.

"*Regemmelech.*"—A man who had this name, and he brought his men with him; and that is what is meant by the words, "and his men." These came to Jerusalem to pray before the Lord, for the children of the captivity had sent by their hand to make inquiry, and to say to the priests and the prophets, "Shall I weep?"

3. "*To speak to the priests* ——— *in the house of the*

* As our translators have it.

† See this passage quoted above, chap. iii. 5, p. 36.

‡ Our translation has *And*.

Lord."—לְבֵית is the same as בְּבֵית. Jonathan has, "Who serve in the temple of the Lord."*

"*And to the prophets.*"—Haggai, Zechariah, and Malachi. But Jonathan has "to the scribes."

"*Should I weep?*"—For as yet they did not believe in the building of the temple, on account of the enemies who had caused the work to cease for many years; and now, although they had heard that they were building, they were weak in faith, and did not wish to go up from Babylon, for they did not believe that the building of the temple would be finished and would stand because of these enemies; they therefore asked whether they should fast on the 9th of Av, as they had done during the seventy years.

"*Separating myself.*"—הִנָּזֵר is the infinitive. The meaning is, "Shall I separate myself from eating, and drinking, and delights." Jonathan has interpreted it, "Shall I withhold myself from delights."

3. "*Then came the word of the Lord.*"—Here it is said, "In the fifth† month, and in the seventh‡ month,"

* So our translators have rendered it.

† The fast of the 5th month happens on the 9th day of the month. The reason why the Jews fast on this day are thus given by Maimonides:—"On the ninth of Av, five things happened. 1st. The decree went forth in the wilderness that the people should not enter the land. 2d. The first and second temple were both destroyed on this day. 3d. The great city Bither was taken, in which were thousands and myriads of Israel; and they had a great king, whom all Israel and the greatest of the wise men thought was the King Messiah: but, 4th, he fell into the hands of the Gentiles, and they were all put to death, and the affliction was great, even like the desolation of the house of the sanctuary. 5th. On that day, devoted to punishment, the wicked Turnus Rufus ploughed up the sanctuary and the parts about, to fulfil that which was said, 'Zion shall be ploughed as a field.'" (Mich. iii. 12.) (Jad Hachasakah. Hilchoth Taanith., c. 5.)

‡ The fast of the seventh is that of the 3d day of Tisri. The Jews fast on this day, "Because on it Gedaliah the son of Ahikam was slain, and thus was quenched the coal of Israel that had been left." (Ibid. See also Jer. xli. 2.)

although there were four fasts.* He names the fifth month, because in it the desolation took place: and he names the seventh month, because in it Gedaliah was killed, and that was a second desolation, for the poor of the land had already been left, and it was not desolate so long as the poor of the people remained whom Nebuzar Adan left as vine-dressers and husbandmen. (Jer. lii. 16). Gedaliah was slain on the first of the seventh month, and as this was a holiday, they appointed the fast for the following day.

"*Did ye at all fast unto me?*"—צַמְתֻּנִי is for צַמְתֶּם אוֹתִי, that is to say, did ye fast on my account? On account of your sins the temple is destroyed, and ye are in captivity, and therefore ye fast: if ye will do judgment and justice, ye need not fast, for the temple shall be built, and go up from the captivity, and ye shall dwell in the land for ever: if ye will do that which is good in my eyes, ye shall not be led away captive from it for ever. The meaning of אָנִי after צַמְתֻּנִי is, "Did I command you to fast?" Jonathan has rendered it thus: "Is it the fast of affliction wherewith ye afflict yourselves before me?"

6. "*And when ye did eat.*"—He means to say, what have I from your feasting or your eating? When ye fast it is because of your sins, and when ye eat and drink it is for your own profit: the whole matter is for yourselves; but what have I in all this, for neither in the fasting nor the eating is there any thing for my glory?

7. "*Should ye not hear the words.*"—What but your

* Besides the two fasts here mentioned, there are two other great fasts mentioned in the 8th chapter; that of the fourth month, or 17th day of Tammuz, on which, according to Maimonides, five evils happened. "1st. The stone tables were broken. 2d. The daily offering ceased in the first temple. 3d. A breach was effected in the walls of Jerusalem at the second destruction. 4th. The wicked Apostomos burned the law; and, 5th, set up an image in the sanctuary." (Ibid.)

The other fast is that of the tenth month, or 10th day of Teveth, on which day "The wicked Nebuchadnezzar, King of Babylon, laid siege to Jerusalem." (Ibid.)

own sins has caused you to fast? for when Jerusalem was in prosperity, I cried by the hand of my servants the prophets that ye should turn from your sins, that the land might not be wasted; but ye did not choose to hear.

"*When men inhabited the south and the plain*," i. e., all the land was dwelling securely, and he mentions the south and the plain to show that if this was the case, much more was there a secure dwelling in the mountains and hills.

יֹשֵׁב the active participle here means that there was in them a secure dwelling.

8. "*And the word of the Lord came.*"—After the parenthesis about "inhabiting the plain and the south," he returns to conclude the former things, that he should tell all the people of the land, what the former prophets who spoke to them had cried.

9. "*Thus speaketh the Lord of hosts* ——— *execute true judgment.*"—When ye judge between man and man, let your judgment be the judgment of truth; and with him that has need of it, do mercy and compassion, for they are more than judgment."

10. "*And the widow.*"—Take good heed to yourselves that ye oppress not the weak, either in their property or by words.

"*Evil of a man against his brother*," i. e., do not think evil one against another in your heart; even the thought is forbidden, how much more the deed, and further, the thought which leads to the deed. And even though he does not commit it, it is forbidden, for it is said, "Thou shalt not hate thy brother in thy heart."

11. "*But they refused* ——— *and gave a backsliding shoulder.*"—סֹרֶרֶת signifies "to turn away from;" as in Hos. iv. 16, "As a backsliding (perverse) heifer," for he that does not wish to attend to him that calls him, turns away his shoulder, and will not turn towards him.

12. "*They made their hearts as an adamant.*"—שָׁמִיר, an adamant is a hard stone which no iron can cut.

"*And the words which the Lord.*"—The words of reproof which the prophets spake to them.

"*In his Spirit.*"—In the spirit of prophecy which was speaking along with the prophets.

"*Therefore came a great wrath.*"—Upon your fathers.

13. "*It is come to pass as he cried.*"—As he cried to them in my name, and they did not hear, so they will cry and he will not hear.

14. "*But I scattered them with a whirlwind amongst all the nations whom they knew not.*" The word וָאֵסָעֲרֵם presents a grammatical difficulty. It has been said that it is a form compounded of Kal* and Niphal.† My lord my father has written that it is altogether from Kal, and although it is solitary,‡ the meaning is, "And I will be scattered with them" עמם; as in Isa. xxxv. 1, יְשֻׂשׂוּם מִדְבָּר וְצִיָּה, "The wilderness and solitary place shall be glad *with* them," עמם. The punctuation is וָאֵסָעֲרֵם, and not וָאֶסְעָרֵם, in order to make wide § the ע and to make it light, and they have pointed the א with Tzere and the Samech with Kametz, to make the word still longer and

* Michlal Jophi reads Kal and Pihel.

† Gesenius and Rosenmüller both explain this peculiar punctuation as a Syriasm. The former says, "In the Syriac, where the vowel-letters are much more liquid, than in the Hebrew, the letters א and י at the beginning of words are often allowed to quiesce. For so one may call the Syriac custom of pronouncing א and י with Sheva at the beginning of words as a simple vowel-sound, E and I, when at the same time the full vowel is written; as ܐܶܡܰܪ: he said, for אֱמַר ܐܰܠܳܗܳܐ: God ܝܺܠܶܕ he bare. In Hebrew this has been imitated in the case of א, which, instead of (-:) and (∵:), gets Zere, and instead of (т:), gets Cholem. E.g., אֵסָעֲרֵם instead of אֲסַעֲרֵם, Zech. vii. 14; אֵרוֹמֵם instead of אֲרוֹמֵם, Isa. xxxiii. 10; אֵפוֹ instead of אֱפוֹ, Exod. xvi. 23; אֵתָיוּ instead of אֱתָיוּ, Isaiah xxi. 12; &c. (Gesen. Lehrgebäude. p. 151, 152.) See Rosenmüller Schol. in loc.

‡ Intransitive. See Buxtorf in בודד.

§ This is to facilitate the pronunciation.

easier. The meaning of the whole is, "I will be afflicted with them" in captivity, similar to the declaration, "In all their afflictions he was afflicted." The law speaks after the manner of men.* But it is more correct to interpret ואסערם as a transitive verb, for we find that sometimes a verb is both transitive and intransitive, as for instance, the verb הלם is intransitive, in Judges v. 22:— אָז הָלְמוּ עִקְּבֵי־סוּס, "Then were the horsehoofs broken;" and is transitive in Proverbs xxiii. 35, הֲלָמוּנִי בַּל יָדָעְתִּי, "They have beaten me, and I felt it not." The wise man R. Abraham Aben Ezra, of blessed memory, has interpreted, "I will storm upon them with my storm of wind," i. e., he scattered them over the face of all nations.

"*Thus the land was desolate after them.*"—The contrary of "The south and the plains were inhabited."

* Thus far Joseph Kimchi.

CHAPTER VIII.

1. "*Again the word of the Lord of hosts came, saying.*"—The same as if it were written, "came *to me*, saying."* And in the Masorah it is said, there is no similar case.

2. "*Thus saith the Lord.*"—This chapter contains comfort for the time to come, in the days of Messiah, in the wars of Gog and Magog, who shall come against Jerusalem. But at that time I will be jealous for her with great jealousy, and I will pour out great wrath upon all the heathen who come against her.

3. "*Thus saith ——— and Jerusalem shall be called a city of truth.*"—As he promised, "The remnant of Israel shall not do iniquity, nor speak lies:" (Zeph. iii. 13.) This is a declaration for all the land of Israel, but he mentions Jerusalem as it is the capital of the kingdom, and also because of the mountain of the Lord, the holy mountain, which strangers shall no more profane.

4. "*Thus saith the Lord.*"—With reference to all the comfort, he says, "Thus saith," to give force to the consolation, for the good here promised shall be in every way.

"*And every man with his staff in his hand,*" to be taken literally, as is said, "for very age."

5. "*And the streets.*"—This is plain.

6. "*Thus saith the Lord ——— should it be marvellous in mine eyes.*"—Some interpreters explain this interrogatively, as if he had said, "Should it also be wonderful in mine eyes." As the words אַתָּה זֶה בְּנִי עֵשָׂו, "Art thou my very son Esau?" (Gen. xxvii. 24), and other similar passages. But the wiseman R. Abraham Aben Ezra takes it as it stands, and to mean, "I will do a

* So it is in English.

wonderful thing in those days, of which I never did the like."

7. "*Thus saith ——— from the east country and from the west country;*" i. e., the whole world, for Israel has been scattered in every part of the world.

8. "*And I will bring them ——— in the midst of Jerusalem.*"—He mentions Jerusalem, as I have explained above, because it was the city of the royal residence, and on account of the temple whither all Israel was accustomed to come.

"*In truth.*"—Similar to the promise, "I will betroth thee unto me in faithfulness." (Hosea ii. 22, English 20.)

9. "*Thus let your hands be strong.*"—As ye hear all these future consolations, let your hands be strong in the commandments of God and to build the temple, according as ye have begun, for ye see that in the day that the foundation of the temple was laid the blessing began to come upon you.

10. "*For before these days;*" i. e., Before the foundation of the temple was laid, which was in the second year of Darius, on the 24th day of the ninth month, ye know that the hire of man did not become (לא נהיה), that is to say, did not become a blessing, but turned to a curse.

"*And the hire of beast was not.*"—אֵינֶנָּה, as if the beast was not when its hire turned to a curse.

"*For I set.*"—וָאֲשַׁלַּח signifies permitting a thing for evil, as וְהִשְׁלַחְתִּי בָכֶם אֶת חַיַּת שָׂדֶה, "I will also send wild beasts among you" (Lev. xxvii. 22); as the Targum has "I excited every man."

11. "*But now.*"—This is clear.

12. "*For the seed peace;*"* that is to say, Your seed shall be peace and a blessing, so that they will call it "a seed of peace." Jonathan's interpretation is, "The seed shall be perfect."

"*And I will cause the remnant of this people to*

* See marginal translation.

possess."—It is possible that this may have been spoken of the second temple, on condition that they would keep the commandments of the Lord; or it is still future, referring to the days of Messiah; and this is proved by the following verse, which says, "O house of Judah, and house of Israel." During the second temple the house of Israel did not return.

13. "*And it shall be as ye were a curse.*"—For the Gentiles curse you, yea in every famine or misfortune that comes upon this land, they say it is on account of the sin of the Israelites dwelling amongst them.

"*And ye shall be a blessing.*"—For the Gentiles shall be blessed in you, like Gen. xii. 2, "And thou shalt be a blessing."

"*Let your hands be strong.*"—At this time, on account of the good consolations which, ye hear, are to come upon Israel.

14. "*For thus saith the Lord —— and I repented not.*"—For I did what I intended, even to the desolation of their land, and the leading them into captivity.

15. "*Fear ye not.*"—Because of those that resist you, Sanballat and his companions, who think to cause your work to cease now.

16. "*These are the things —— speak ye truth.*"—Speak not with one thing in your mouth and another thing in your heart.

"*And the judgment of peace.*"—וּמִשְׁפַּט שָׁלוֹם, for if ye judge righteousness there will be peace between the parties in the lawsuit, according as our rabbies have said in a proverb of the children of men. "He that has his coat taken from him by the tribunal, let him sing and go his way."* And they have adduced in proof that verse,

* Talm. Bab. Sanhedrin, fol. 7, col. i., about the middle of the page. Rashi explains "that he is to sing and go his way, because they have judged the judgment of truth, and have taken away that which would have been stolen property if he retained."

"And all this people shall also go to their place in peace." (Exod. xviii. 23.) "All the people," even he that is condemned in judgment. And our rabbies, of blessed memory, have interpreted ומשפט שלום of reconciliation, for it is said, "What sort of judgment is that in which there is peace? They answered, That of arbitration."* וּמִשְׁפַּט is pointed with pathach, because it is in regimen.

"*In your gates.*"—For that was the seat of the elders; as it is said in the law, "To the gate to the elders." (Deut. xxv. 7.)

17. "*And let none of you imagine evil against his neighbour.*"—The same is said above (vii. 10), and there it is interpreted.

"*And love no false oath.*"—And afterwards he says, "That I hate;" that is to say, Do not ye love that which I hate.

"*For all these are things.*"—Imagining evil against a neighbour and false oaths, and that which is the opposite of the former things; i.e., Truth and peace. Therefore he says, "All these things."

18. "*And the word of the Lord came to me.*"—If ye will do these things which I have commanded you, the God of hosts says, that the fasts concerning which ye have asked whether ye shall fast on those days, ye shall not fast, but ye shall rejoice in them, because of the abundance of good which shall be to you.

19. "*The fast of the fourth month.*"—This is Tammuz in which they fasted in captivity, on the 17th of the

* i.e., Where the parties are brought to agree by means of arbitration. The whole passage is found in Sanhedrin, fol. 6, col. 2:—"R. Judah ben Korcha says, it is a commandment to put an end to a suit by arbitration; for it is said, 'Judge truth and the judgment of peace in your gates.' (Zech. viii. 16.) But how can there be peace in a place where there is judgment; or in a place where there is peace, how can there be judgment? The difficulty is solved by considering what sort of judgment is here intended: it is that of arbitration."

month, the day on which a breach was effected in the city.

"*The fast of the fifth month.*"—This is Av, in which they fasted on the 9th day.†

"*The fast of the seventh month.*"—This is the fast of Gedaliah, as we interpreted above.

"*The fast of the tenth month.*"—This is the tenth of Tevath, on which day the King of Babylon invested Jerusalem.

"*Shall be.*"—Every one of them shall be to the house of Judah during the second temple, for the ten tribes have not returned.

"*Therefore love the truth and peace.*"—And on condition that ye love the truth and peace, as I have commanded you.

20. "*Thus saith the Lord ——— there shall come people.*"—There shall yet be a time when the people shall come, and this will be in the days of Messiah. עוֹד has the same signification as in עוֹד הַיּוֹם גָּדוֹל, "It is yet high day:" and again, אוֹשִׁיבְךָ בָאֳהָלִים, "I will yet make thee to dwell in tabernacles" (Hos. xii. 10, English 9): and other similar passages.

21. "*I will go also.*"—According to its Targum, "One shall say to the other, I will go also."

22. "*Yea, many people and strong nations.*"—Strong in number: and we find this sense of עָצַם in Jer. xv. 8: "Their widows are strong (are increased) to me above the sand of the seas." It here refers to the matter of quantity. The same sentiment is repeated in different words. The Targum of Jonathan has "great kingdoms."

23. "*Thus saith the Lord ——— in those days that ten men shall take hold.*"—This that I have said to you shall happen in those days when they shall take hold. And afterwards these words, "even shall take hold," are

* See the notes above on chapter vii. 3.

repeated on account of the length of the intervening sentence, as the words, אם באמת ובתמים, "If truly and sincerely," are repeated in Judges ix. 16—19. There are many such passages.

"*Ten men.*"—Ten is not to be taken strictly, but it is a round number, like "*Ten women shall bake your bread,*" and other similar passages. And according to the Drash, "Ten men out of all languages of the nations" means 700 to each skirt of the Arbah Kanphoth* (four corners).

* So the Jews call that particular garment on which they wear the fringes commanded in Numbers xv. 38, 39.

CHAPTER IX.

1. " *The burden of the word of the Lord in the land of Hadrach.*" —This prophecy refers to the land of Hadrach and Damascus, for there shall be its resting-place; or, the interpretation is, The prophecy of the Lord shall yet be in the land of Hadrach as in the land of Israel, for it shall be (a part) of the land of Israel, and thus Damascus shall be his resting-place, i. e., the Shechinah (habitation) of his glory and his prophecy. We find in the words of our rabbies, of blessed memory, that " R. Benaiah says, that חדרך, Hadrach, is the Messiah, who is sharp, חד, to the Gentiles, and tender, רך, to Israel. R. Jose, the son of a Damascus woman, said to him, How long wilt thou pervert the Scriptures against us? I call heaven and earth to witness, that I am from Damascus, and there is there a place, of which the name is Hadrach. He said to him, And what do I establish by the words, ' *Damascus shall be his resting-place?*' I establish this, that Jerusalem shall yet extend as far as Damascus, for it is said, ' His resting-place,' and he has no rest but Jerusalem, as he says, ' This is my rest for ever and ever.' (Ps. cxxxii. 14.) He said to him, And what do I establish by the words, ' And the city shall be built upon her heap?' (Jer. xxx. 18.) He said to him, That she shall not be moved from her place. He said to him, And what do I prove by the words, ' It was made broader, and went round still upward?' (Ezek. xli. 7.) That Jerusalem shall be enlarged and extend on all sides, as this fig-tree, which is narrow underneath, and broad above, and the gates of Jerusalem shall yet extend to Damascus, and so it is said, ' Thy nose is as the tower of Lebanon, that looketh towards Damascus,' and the captivities come

and encamp in the midst of it, as it is said, 'And Damascus his resting place.'" *

"*For to the Lord the eye of man.*"—For in those days the eye of all mankind shall be to the Lord, not to idols and images; therefore the land of Hadrach and Damascus, and the other places near the land of Israel, such as Tyre, Sidon, and Hamath, and the cities of the Philistines, shall be included among the cities of Judah, and shall be in the faith of Israel.

"*And all the tribes of Israel,*" and, *á fortiori*, the tribes of Israel shall have their eye and their heart toward the Lord. Or, the meaning of it may be, The eye of man shall be to the Lord, and to all the tribes of Israel to walk in their ways, as is said above, "We will go with you."

2. "*And Hamath also.*"—He says, "And Hamath also;" for it is a great city, as is said, "Hamath Rabbah," and it is outside the border of the land of Israel, for it is one of the borders of the land of Israel; and he says that, at that time Hamath shall be within her border, and that is what is said, "And Hamath also shall border *in her*, Tyre and Zidon, though it be very wise." And thus, also, Tyre and Zidon, which are also in her vicinity, shall be in the midst of her border. "Although she be very wise," refers to Tyre, as is mentioned in Ezekiel's chapter about Tyre (xxvii), and the meaning is, "Although she was wise in her own eyes in former days, her wisdom did not profit her. But in the days of Messiah she shall not trust in her wisdom, but shall humble herself before Israel."

3. "*And Tyre did build herself a strong hold.*"—For although a strong hold was built for her in ancient days, and she heaped up silver as dust, and fine gold as the mire of the streets, all this did not profit her.

* This rabbinical interpretation is to be found with some slight variations in the Yalkut Shimoni, part i. fol. 258, col. 2.

4. "*Behold, the Lord will cast her out,*" i.e., will dispossess her of all her greatness.

"*And he will smite her power in the sea,*" as is explained at large in Ezekiel. And when she shall think of all these things, she shall be humbled in the days of Messiah. For although there were inhabitants in her at that time, they were not the same as the inhabitants in ancient times. The affair of Tyre is known to every one, for it is written in the prophets, and there are also written accounts amongst the Nazarenes who dwell there at this day, and they were there at that time.

5. "*Ashkelon shall see.*"—תֵּרֶא is milra, the accent is on the Resh. He says, when Ashkelon shall see that Tyre is humbled, she will be humbled also. But the true interpretation of the words "Tyre and Zidon," is to connect them with the following verse.

*2. "*And Tyrus did build herself.*"—It is said Hamath shall border therein, but Tyre and Zidon shall be considered as opposing Israel, because she was very wise in her own eyes, as it is written in the book of Ezekiel, and Zidon was near to her, and followed her, therefore it is joined with Tyre.

"*And she did build.*"—She will think to be delivered by the building which she shall build, and by the silver and gold which she shall amass. But all this will not help her, for behold the Lord will cast her out.

"*A strong hold.*"—מָצוֹר, a strong tower, and thus in 2 Chron. xiv. 5 (6), וַיִּבֶן עָרֵי מְצוּרָה, "And he built fenced cities;" Jonathan has also interpreted, "And Tyre has built a strong place for herself."

"*Fine gold.*"—חָרוּץ signifies gold, as בִּירַקְרַק חָרוּץ, "with yellow gold (Psalm lxviii. 14) [13], and so Jonathan has interpreted it.

4. "*The Lord will cast her out,*" יוֹרִשֶׁנָּה.—This verb

* Kimchi here returns to give another interpretation.

has the signification of driving out and sending away, as מוֹרִישׁ אוֹתָם מִפָּנֶיךָ, "He driveth them out before thee," and other similar passages; and so Jonathan renders it, מתרך לה.

"*And he will smite her power in the sea.*"—All the wealth and all the money in which she was trusting, the sea shall come and overwhelm it.

"*And she shall be burned with fire.*"—And she, i. e., the city and her buildings, and her fortified towers, in which she was trusting, a fire shall go forth from the midst of her that shall consume them.

5. "*Ashkelon shall see.*"—And when Ashkelon shall see that Tyre is wasted by the hand of God, she shall fear and humble herself before Israel, and so with Gaza and Ekron.

"*For he hath made ashamed her expectation.*"*—מֶבָּטָהּ, that is Tyre, to which they were looking, מַבִּיטִים, and thought to be saved with her on account of her strength.

מֶבָּטָהּ.—The Mem has a segol.

וְהוֹבִישׁ comes from בּוֹשׁ, to be ashamed.—And the meaning is, They shall be ashamed along with Tyre, to which they were looking, when God, blessed be He, shall cast her out. But Jonathan interprets והוביש, "and shall be ashamed," as referring to Ekron, so that the meaning is, Ekron shall be ashamed of her expectation. His words are, "Behold Ekron is ashamed of the house of his confidence."

"*And the king shall perish from Gaza.*"—Her king who is in her at that time shall perish, and his kingdom also, for it shall be to Israel.

"*And Ashkelon shall not be inhabited.*"—By her men who shall be there at that time, for Israel shall dispose of it.

* The verb וְהוֹבִישׁ may be taken either transitively or intransitively. But the parallel passage in Isaiah xx. 5, "They shall be ashamed of Ethiopia their expectation," shows that it must be taken intransitively.

"*And a bastard shall dwell in Ashdod,*" מַמְזֵר.—Some interpret mamser as the name of a nation. Some say it means a bastard, proceeding from the forbidden intercourse of those Israelites who dwelt alone in the cities of the Philistines, and were separate from the congregation. And, behold, our rabbies have said, that Elijah will cleanse these bastards, and cause them to enter into the congregation of the Lord. But it ought to be interpreted as if the כְּ, the sign of comparison, had been omitted, and thus ממזר means the same as זר, "a stranger." As "a bastard shall not enter." (Deut. xxiii. 2.) And the two Mems are added, as in the word מַמְּגֻרוֹת, "the barns are broken down." (Joel i. 17.) And the meaning is, He of the Philistines that dwelleth in Ashdod, shall dwell there as a man that is a stranger and an alien, for they shall be under the power of Israel, and this is what follows, "I will cut off the pride of the Philistines."

7. "*And I will take away his blood out of his mouth.*" —After the manner of a parable, that is to say, The devouring and consuming of Israel are to be considered as "his blood and abominations,"* that is, I will destroy the wicked of heart who are amongst them, and "he that remaineth shall be for our God," and as to them that remain of them, whose heart is right with the Lord, I will cause him to remain, and he shall be as a governor in Judah. And there is also an interpretation, As the remainder of the sons of the stranger who join themselves to the Lord, for of them it is said, "Even them will I bring to my holy mountain; and make them joyful in my house of prayer." (Isaiah lvi. 7.) Behold they shall be as a governor and as a great man in Israel.

* Hengstenberg gives the true sense of this passage. He says, that "the blood and abominations" here stand for idolatry, as the heathen used to drink the blood of the victims, or to mix it with wine. The meaning then, is, I will turn them from idolatry to worship the true God. (Christologie, part ii. p. 117.) Aben Ezra, in his Commentary, suggests the same interpretation.

"*And Ekron as a Jebusite.*"—Ekron shall be as the Jebusite, the inhabitant of Jerusalem, for the Jebusite was dwelling in the midst of the children of Israel, and was their tributary servant; so it shall be in the days of Messiah. He mentions Judah, because there was the holy mountain and the house of prayer. And our rabbies, of blessed memory, have interpreted, "His blood and his abominations," of the obscene language to which the nations of the world are accustomed.

8. "*And I will encamp about mine house because of the army,*" מִצָּבָה.—This word is here written with ה instead of א.

"*For now have I seen with mine eyes.*"—Now in this time when all this promise shall be accomplished, I have seen with mine eyes their affliction and their deportation into captivity amongst the nations, and I will help them, and will bring upon them all this good. "And I have seen," is similar to "And God saw the children of Israel." (Exod. ii.) But the wise man, R. Abraham Aben Ezra, of blessed memory, has explained, that these are the words of the prophet, who says, "Now have I seen all this with my eyes, in the visions of the night, in prophecy."

9. "*Rejoice greatly, O daughter of Zion,*" גִּילִי is milra.—He mentions the daughter of Jerusalem, because she is the head of the kingdom.

"*Righteous, and having salvation,*" נוֹשָׁע (or saved).—He shall be righteous, and in his righteousness he shall be saved from the sword of Gog and Magog. נוֹשַׁע is pointed with pathach,* for it is the perfect tense turned into the future by the ו conversive.

עָנִי, the same as עָנָיו, "lowly." The Targum of Jonathan has עִנְוְתָן, "humble, lowly, meek." And so it is said in the prophecies of Isaiah, "He shall not cry, nor lift up, nor cause his voice to be heard in the street. A bruised reed, &c." (Isaiah xlii. 2, 3.)

* It is not so pointed in the present copies.

"*And riding upon an ass.*"—Not from poverty, for behold the whole world shall be in his power, but from humility he will ride upon an ass: and further, to show that Israel shall not want horse nor chariot, therefore it is added, "And I will cut off the chariot from Ephraim, and the horse from Jerusalem."

"*And upon a colt, the foal of an ass.*"—The same sentence is repeated in other words. And, further, he mentions "a colt," because it is young, and particularly selected for riding; and so it is said of the sons of Ibzan, "that ride upon thirty ass colts." (Judges x. 4, and xii. 8.)

"*The foal of she-asses,*" בן אתונות, i. e., the foal of one of the she-asses. A similar idiom is found in וַיִּקָּבֵר בְּעָרֵי גִלְעָד, "And was buried in the cities of Gilead." (Judges xii. 7), i. e., in one of the cities of Gilead.

10. "*And I will cut off.*—And so it is said in the prophecy of Micah, v. 10, "And I will cut off the horses out of the midst of thee, and I will destroy thy chariots." Ephraim and Jerusalem are mentioned, because, in the former days, the kingdom was divided, but in the day of the Messiah they shall be one.

"*And he shall speak peace to the heathen.*"—He shall make peace between one nation and another, if they be at war, for all the Gentiles shall be obedient to him.

"*And his dominion shall be from sea to sea.*"—The wise man, R. Abraham Aben Ezra, of blessed memory, has explained this to mean, "From the south sea, which is called the sea of Edom, to the northern sea, which is the ocean."

"*And from the river to the ends of the earth.*"—From the river that goes forth from Edom, which is in the beginning of the east, to the ends of the earth, which is the end of the west. And, behold, he shall rule in all the world.

11. "*As for thee also.*"—This he says in reference to

the congregation of Israel. As it is said of the King, the Messiah, that he shall be saved by his righteousness, so it is said, As for thee, thou shalt be saved by the blood of thy covenant, and that is the blood of circumcision, which Israel in captivity has adhered to more tenaciously than to all the commandments.

" *Out of the pit wherein is no water.*"—This is the captivity. Some interpret the words, " By the blood of thy covenant," as referring to the blood of the covenant which the Lord made with Israel in Sinai. Our rabbies, of blessed memory, have said, that " water " means prophecy figuratively; for prophecy has never existed during the captivity, and there has been no prophet after Haggai, Zechariah, and Malachi. And we find a similar passage referring to prophecy, " Ho, every one that thirsteth, Come ye to the waters." (Isaiah lv.)

12. " *Turn ye to the strong hold.*"—The commentators have interpreted this paragraph as referring to the second temple. And our rabbies, of blessed memory, have done the same, except that they interpret half this verse of the future, as written above. The meaning of " Turn ye to the strong hold," is, Turn ye to God, blessed be He, for he is a strong hold and a tower of strength.

" *Ye prisoners of hope.*"—Because they had been in captivity, and had been prisoners, but had hoped for the redemption these many years.

12. " *Even to-day do I declare that I will render double unto thee.*" * The blessed God says, In another message, which is near at hand, the prophet, the announcer, will declare a second message, after that first one relating to the future. And this is God's deliverance of Israel from the Greeks by the hand of Mattathias, the son of John, the high-priest, and by the hands of his sons in the time of the second temple. But in my opinion

* Kimchi appears to have construed this verse thus, " Even to-day I will cause to return to thee an announcer of a second."

this whole paragraph is future; I will, however, interpret it, first, according to the opinion of the commentators, of the second temple.

13. "*When I have bent.*"—The tribe of Judah is my bow, which I will bend against Greece, i. e., By means of Judah, I will make war with Greece.

"*Filled the bow with Ephraim.*"—This expression is similar to "And Jehu filled his hand with the bow" (2 Kings ix. 24), and it means the stretching of the bow with all his force to shoot the arrow. And Ephraim is mentioned, for although in the second temple there was neither the tribe of Ephraim nor the other tribes, yet there remained in the land after the captivity, in the days of Hoshea, these few, as we find in the words of Josiah, "From the coast of Manasseh and Ephraim, and all the remnant of Israel." And these went into captivity with the tribe of Judah and Benjamin, to Babylon, and returned with them when they returned.

"*And raised up thy sons, O Zion, against thy sons, O Greece.*"—I will stir them up against them, and will put strength and power in them, and this is what is said, "And made thee as the sword of a mighty man."

14. "*And the Lord shall be seen over them,*" i. e., The Lord shall fight for them.

"*And the Lord God shall blow the trumpet.*"—As if he should blow the trumpet, after the manner of warriors.

"*And shall go with the whirlwinds of the south.*"—He shall go against the children of Greece like a whirlwind, as it is written, "The Lord hath his way in the whirlwind and the storm." (Nahum i. 3.) תֵּימָן is mentioned, that is the south point, for thence comes the whirlwind, as it is written, "Out of the chamber cometh the whirlwind." (Job xxxvii. 9.) And חדר means the south, as it is written, וְחַדְרֵי תֵמָן, "And the chambers of the south." (Job ix. 9.) Jonathan also has thus rendered it, "And he shall lead with a storm of wind from the south."

15. "*The Lord of Hosts shall defend them.*"—Judah and Ephraim, whom he had mentioned.

"*And they shall eat and subdue the slingstones.*"—Not enough that the Lord shall defend them, so that their enemies shall not subdue them, but they shall consume (lit. eat) their enemies, and shall subdue those that are left for servants and handmaids. The children of Greece are called slingstones, which are common stones, with which the slingers sling; whereas the children of Judah are called "stones of a crown," which are precious stones and pearls, which they place in a crown.

"*And they shall drink and make a noise through wine,*" that is, they drink the blood of their enemies, and shall make a noise over them as if they were drinking wine, and this is similar to that passage, "And they shall be drunken with their own blood." (Isaiah xlix. 26.) And the making a noise over wine is similar to "They are drunken, but not with wine. They make a noise,* but not with strong drink." (Isaiah xxix. 9.)

"*And they shall be filled like a bowl, like the corners of the altar.*"—They shall be full of the blood of their enemies as a bowl in which they receive the blood of the sacrifices, or, as the corners of the altar, which they sprinkled with blood.

16. "*And the Lord God shall save them as the flock of his people.*"—Just as a man saves his flock with all his strength, so he will save his people, for they are his flock. Some interpreters say, As Moses saved them, for he fed them as a flock, as it is written, "Thou leddest thy people like a flock by the hand of Moses and Aaron." (Psalm lxxvii. 20, Heb. 21.)

"*For they shall be as the stones of a crown lifted up as an ensign upon his land.*"—Judah and Ephraim shall be as the stones of a crown lifted up and exalted upon his land, which is the Holy Land. מִתְנוֹסְסוֹת is the

* Kimchi read הָמוּ, whereas we read נָעוּ, they stagger.

same as מִתְרוֹמְמוֹת, "lifted up," as נָתַתָּה לִּירֵאֶיךָ נֵּס לְהִתְנוֹסֵס, "Thou hast given a banner to them that feared thee, that it may be lifted up." (Psalm lx. 6, English 4.) In like manner נֵס, a standard, has reference to lifting up and exaltation, for the standard-bearer lifts up and exalts it above the heads of the people.

17. "*How great is his goodness, and how great is his beauty.*"—How good is the fruit of their land, how good is the corn and new wine, which make to grow and bring up such handsome young men and maidens, as shall be at that time.

OBSERVATIONS IN DEFENCE OF THE CHRISTIAN INTERPRETATION OF CHAPTER IX.

As this chapter contains a passage, quoted in the New Testament as having been fulfilled by an event in the history of the Lord Jesus Christ, it requires a special consideration. There are two questions to be considered; First, The general meaning of the prophecy; and Secondly, The applicability to Jesus of Nazareth.

1. The New Testament takes for granted that the subject is Messianic, for it cites the passage to prove the Messiahship of our blessed Lord; but the question here arises, whether the Jews of that day, and in the succeeding times, have admitted that the chapter refers to the Messiah, or whether this is a private interpretation peculiar to the New Testament? * The writings of the Jews furnish an unbroken chain of testimony to prove that it was always referred to the Messiah, and that, therefore, the writers of the New Testament did not lay

* Theodoret says, that the Jews of his time interpreted the passage of Zerubbabel, but there is no trace of this exposition in any of the Jewish writings. (Hengstenberg Christologie, part ii. p. 141.)

hold of a text, the letter of which seemed to suit their purpose, but applied a passage of Scripture which the Jewish nation ever regarded as a test to try the claims of every pretender to the Messiahship.

The book of Zohar shows us the opinion of the Jews in the first century of Christianity. Speaking of Abraham's saddling his ass, it says, "And on his account it is said of Messiah, Lowly, and riding upon an ass."* And in a subsequent passage, "On this account it is written of the Messiah, Lowly and riding upon an ass."† The Talmud shows us that this interpretation continued in later ages, "R. Joshua, the son of Levi objects, that it is written in one place, 'Behold, one like the Son of Man came with the clouds of heaven:' but in another place it is written, 'Lowly, and riding upon an ass.' The solution is, if they be righteous, he shall come with the clouds of heaven. If they be not righteous, he shall come lowly and riding upon an ass." ‡

At a later period Saadiah Gaon, in interpreting the above-cited words of Daniel, says, "This is the Messiah our righteousness. But is it not written of the Messiah, 'Lowly and riding upon an ass?' Yes, but this shows that he will come in humility, and not in pride upon horses."§

The first trace of a different interpretation occurs in the 12th century. Aben Ezra tells us, in his commentary on the passage, that "R. Moses the priest says, this refers to Nehemiah, the Tirshatha, of whom it is written in Ezra, 'There is a King in Judah' (Nehem. vi. 7);

* ובגיניה אתמר על משיח עני ורוכב על חמור. (Lublin Edit. of the Zohar, folio 110, col. 3, of part iii.)

† ובגין דא כתיב ביה במשיח עני ורוכב על חמור. (Fol. 133, col. 4. See other passages from this book in Schöttgen, vol. ii. p. 20.)

‡ Talm. Bab. Sanhedrin, fol. 98, col. 1.

§ וזהו משיח צדקנו והלא כתוב על משיח עני ורוכב על חמור אלא יבוא בענוה כי לא יבוא על סוסים בגאות.

therefore it is said, 'Lowly and riding upon an ass.' A horse is not mentioned, for he was too poor to buy one." This opinion, however, Aben Ezra immediately rejects and refutes. He says, "This is not true; for Nehemiah was governor, and did not require the bread of the governor from Israel, and yet every day entertained a great number of persons at his table. (Nehem. vi. 15—18.) And how is it that he should not have a horse?" To which it may also be added, that Nehemiah never assumed the style and title of royalty; and when Sanballat accused him of it, he replied, "There are no such things as thou sayest; but thou feignest them out of thine own heart."

Aben Ezra goes on, however, to give his own interpretation, saying, "According to my opinion, this king is Judas the son of the Hasmonean, for he was a mighty man, as it is written, 'I have made thee as a sword of a mighty man' (Zech. ix. 13); and his hand was mighty against the Greeks, but at first he had neither wealth nor horses." But this opinion does not appear to have found any favourers amongst the Jews, and Abarbanel has saved us the trouble of refuting it. He says, "I am astonished at the wicked motive that blinded his understanding, for Judas, the son of the Hasmonean, was never called King all his days; whereas the king, mentioned to Zion by name, is David, who took Zion. Again, if the prophecy refer to the Hasmoneans, why is Ephraim mentioned, for there was no kingdom of Ephraim during the second temple? Moreover, Judas the Hasmonean did not speak peace to all the heathen, neither was his dominion from sea to sea, nor was there in his days any fulfilment of the words, 'When I have fill the bow with Ephraim,' for the kingdom of the ten tribes, called the kingdom of Ephraim, has not returned to this day." (Abarbanel in loc.) Excepting these two writers, all the Jews, ancient and modern, not even excepting that determined opposer of Christianity,

R. Isaac, the author of the Chizzuk Emunah, agree in interpreting this passage of the Messiah; so that, as far as authority goes, the New Testament interpretation is fully justified. The interpretation does not, however, rest solely on authority. There are some distinct declarations which can refer to none but the Messiah. First, that he should speak peace to the heathen; second, that he should be the king of Zion and Redeemer of Israel; and, thirdly, that his dominion should be from sea to sea, and from the river to the ends of the earth. These three conditions have never been fulfilled in any of Israel's ancient kings, and exactly agree with the general tenor of Scripture in describing the Messiah's character.

Having ascertained that the prophecy refers to the Messiah, our next business is to consider the import of some particular passages on which there is a difference of opinion. And first, what are we to understand by the words, "Lowly and riding upon an ass?" Do they intimate a moral quality, humility, or a state of humiliation, or both? Kimchi, as we have seen, says that עָנִי, lowly, is synonymous with עָנָיו, meek, humble. And of "riding upon an ass" he says, "Not from poverty, for behold the whole world shall be in his power, but from humility he shall ride upon an ass: and further, to show that Israel shall not want horse nor chariot." On the other hand, R. Moses, as cited above, interprets עָנִי to signify poor, because, he says, Nehemiah was too poor to buy a horse. And Aben Ezra follows him, saying, that "at first Judas Maccabæus had neither wealth nor horses." Abarbanel leaves the matter undecided, saying, "His salvation shall not be by the strength of the horse, nor by the legs of a man; for he shall be at his commencement lowly and riding upon an ass. But it is also possible to interpret this of humility, as if the word ענו (humble) had been used."* Three out of these four commentators admit

* אבל לא תהיה תשועתו בגבור׳ הסוס ולא בשוקי האי׳ כי הוא יהיה בתחילתו עני ורוכב על חמור וגם אפש׳ לפר׳ עני מלשון ענוה כאלו אמר ענו ׃

that the word may mean "poor." Two say positively that it signifies "poor" in this particular passage, and only one asserts that it signifies "humble." The weight of testimony, then, would incline us to reject the opinion of that one; and this inclination is confirmed by the discovery that these three give an unbiassed opinion, and that the other had a motive for assigning a particular meaning. R. Moses and Aben Ezra applied the passage to individuals whom they might acknowledge to be poor and lowly without compromising their religious views. Abarbanel thought that Messiah might be lowly at first. But not so Kimchi: he applied the passage to the Messiah, and considered it unbecoming his dignity to be poor and lowly; his religious views therefore coloured his interpretation. But an examination of other passages will show that Kimchi is wrong, and that עָנִי and עָנָו are not synonymous, for they cannot be interchanged without changing the sense. For instance: "Thou shalt not oppress an hired servant that is poor and needy, עָנִי וְאֶבְיוֹן." (Deut. xxiv. 14.) Here עָנָו would entirely change the sense. It would be, "Thou shalt not afflict an hired servant who is humble and needy;" which would imply, that if he were proud he might be oppressed, and so one might go through the numerous passages in the Concordance. But Kimchi himself shall bear witness against himself. In his Lexicon, after giving examples of the root עָנָה, he says, "And the adjective [occurs in the following passages] 'Neither did she strengthen the hand of the poor עָנִי and needy.' (Ezek. xvi. 49.) 'The poor הָעֲנִיִּים and needy.' (Isa. xli. 17.) 'O thou afflicted עֲנִיָּה, tossed with tempest, &c.' (Isa. liv. 11.) The substantive [occurs as follows]: 'He hath not despised or abhorred the affliction of the afflicted עֱנוּת עָנִי.' (Ps. xxii. 25, English 24.) And again, another form of the substantive in the words, 'The bread of affliction לֶחֶם עֹנִי' (Deut. xvi. 3), which is so called because they were afflicted in Egypt." Now the reader will observe from these passages, and it is generally true, that עָנִי, poor or afflicted, is usually connected with some word expressive of poverty. He will observe further that the substantives formed from this word do not signify humility, as they ought to do if Kimchi's Commentary were true, but that they both express affliction: and he may gather from the whole that the word signifies "afflicted, in trouble," it may be from poverty, or from other causes. It therefore is not synonymous with עָנָו, humble, the substantive of which, עֲנָוָה, signifies humility. In the passage before us, therefore, the word does not signify "humble," but "in lowly circumstances." It does not exclude humility of mind, on the contrary, as coming from the same root with עָנָו, humble, it has an affinity with it, but it absolutely implies that the person to whom it is applied is "afflicted," or "in lowly circumstances." The English word "lowly," selected by our translators, has the advantage of the double meaning, but it is not sufficiently strong; for a person may be in lowly circumstances without suffering affliction, as this word necessarily implies. The prophet, therefore, tells us that the Messiah should come to Jerusalem in an afflicted and lowly condition, to which the following words, "riding on an ass," exactly agree. A poor and afflicted person riding on an ass, does not excite the idea of grandeur, but of lowliness and poverty: it is, therefore, needless to discuss the second clause, or to answer those passages which show that the judges of Israel rode upon asses. Hengstenberg remarks well, that all these examples are taken from a period antecedent to the reign of Solomon, but that after that monarch had introduced horses not one such instance is to be found. But the discussion is superfluous, the meaning of עָנִי necessarily fixes the sense of the following words.

There is one word more that requires a remark, and that is the word נוֹשָׁע, "having salvation." R. Isaac accuses the Christians of corrupting the text here, saying,

"The Nazarenes have altered the word נוֹשָׁע (saved), and written instead of it מוֹשִׁיעַ (Saviour), in order to add some auxiliary confirmation to their faith." Now in the first place, the accusation as it stands is perfectly false. The Christians have never altered this word. In every Christian edition of the Hebrew Bible it stands, just as it does in those edited by Jews. But in the next place, allowing him to mean, what he does not say, that some Christians, as the Vulgate, have translated the word "Saviour," and not "saved," as he would have it, they did not do this with a fraudulent intention to confirm their faith, but were led by *Jews* to think that this was the right sense of the word. The Jews, who translated Zechariah into Greek, before the rise of Christianity, translated נוֹשָׁע by σώζων, "saving, or Saviour," and Christians simply followed them. The mistake, therefore, is not to be attributed to the Christians, but to the Jews themselves. But if Jews say that the Greek text has been altered, then we refer them to the Targum of Jonathan, who translates the word by פָּרִיק, "Redeemer," or Saviour; and surely Jonathan had no fraudulent desire to favour Christianity. His translation shows that the meaning of the word originated, and was common, amongst the Jews themselves; they, therefore, and not the Christians, are answerable for it. Our English translation has followed the Hebrew, and rendered the word "having salvation:" but if the Jews like the word "saved" better, as being more literal, we have no objection, for it will make no difference in the Christian application of the passage.

Another passage, which demands peculiar consideration, is the latter half of the 12th verse, which our English translators have rendered "Even to-day *do I* declare *that* I will render double to thee." They have here inserted the three words printed in italics, and have connected the word "double," as the accusative, with the verb, "I will render." For this translation they have had authority of the Septuagint, which has *καί ἀντι μιᾶς ἡμέρας παροικεσίας σȣ διπλᾶ ἀνταποδώσω σοι*, "Instead of one day of thy sojourning, I will repay double to thee." The Vulgate has, "hodie quoque annuntians duplicia reddam tibi," which, is, however, much more like the Hebrew, as "duplicia" may be connected either with the preceding or following word. The Targum of Jonathan gives a similar sense: "Even this day will I send to announce to you, that, concerning the double blessings which I promised you, I will bring to you."* How Jonathan construed the original is not very clear, but the sense evidently is, that God would give them the double. But the English version, though resting on such authority, and assumed as the true sense by Hengstenberg,† is certainly not correct; for, in the first place, the accents connect the word "double" with "declare," and not with "render." The literal translation of the text, according to the accents, is, "Even this day: an announcer of double will I cause to return to thee." But this sense, determined by the accents, is confirmed by the usage of the language. The verb הִגִּיד is almost universally followed by an accusative of the thing announced, or a dative of the person, or both. If, then, מַגִּיד be taken in its participial sense, it will require one of the two, but according to the English version it has neither. It is true that מַגִּיד might be taken as a substantive, "an announcer," but then the sense of the whole would be, "I, an announcer, will render double unto thee;" but this sense is far from satisfactory. The reading of the accents is further confirmed by the circumstance, that the words of the text then give a complete sense, without adding a single word for which there is no authority in the original. The English version has added the pronoun "I" and the

* אף יומא דין אשלח לחואה לכון די על חד תרין בטבון די אמרית איתי לכון׃

† He translates "Heute noch zeige ich an: Das Doppelte will ich dir zurückgeben."

connecting word "that." The construing suggested by the accents gives a complete sense without taking any such liberty; and for these reasons I prefer that construction, and think that the whole passage ought to stand thus:—"Turn ye to the strong hold, ye prisoners of hope: even to-day: an announcer of double will I cause to return to thee." In the words "even to-day" I find a parallel to "To-day, if ye will hear his voice" (Ps. xcv.); and by "double" I understand the double portion of blessing which God has promised; as in Isaiah, "For your shame ye shall have double, and for confusion they shall rejoice in their portion: therefore in their land they shall possess the double." (Isa. lxi. 7.) And by the "announcer of double," I understand the Messiah, as he is described in that same chapter: "The Spirit of the Lord God is upon me: because the Lord hath anointed me to preach good tidings to the meek: he hath sent me to bind up the broken-hearted, to proclaim liberty to the captives, and the opening of the prison to them that are bound," &c.; where I also find the same allusion to prison and prisoner. The sense of the whole would be, "Turn in true penitence to the stronghold, that is, to God, ye Jews, prisoners of hope: turn, even to-day, after all your impenitence, and I will cause the Messiah to return to you as the announcer of double blessings."

We now proceed to consider the applicability of the whole to Jesus of Nazareth. The modern Jews say it is no proof of his Messiahship, for that it was not fulfilled in him. The detail of their reasoning is given by R. Isaac, in the Chizzuk Emunah, and this must first be answered.

He says, it cannot apply to Jesus of Nazareth, "For the whole chapter refers to the future, and speaks of the gathering of the captivities of Israel, and the coming of the true Messiah, which we expect in the last days; and

° Wagenseil's Tela Ignea, vol. ii., p. 295.

further, of the promises and joyful declarations of what will happen in his time; according to the intention of the prophecy, if well explained with reference to the preceding and following context. The preceding context is, 'The burden of the word of the Lord, and Damascus shall be the rest thereof,' . . . that is to say, these cities, namely, Hadrach, Damascus, and others, shall, in the time of the Messiah, form a part of the land of Israel, and shall be called the resting-place of the Holy One, blessed be He."

This foundation of all R. Isaac's reasoning is contrary to truth; the whole chapter does not refer to the future. In the verses, to which he refers, the prophet announces the destruction of Tyre and Zidon, which is long since past. The prophet says, "Tyrus did build herself a strong hold, and heaped up silver as the dust, and fine gold as the mire of the streets. Behold, the Lord will cast her out, and he will smite her power in the sea; and she shall be devoured with fire." Now, it is known to every one, that Tyre was destroyed in the time of Alexander the Great, and that from that day to this, she has had neither power nor riches. Kimchi himself says, "The affair of Tyrus is known to every one." And Abarbanel, who absurdly endeavours to prove that Tyrus here means Venice, admits that, "The Tyre that was close to the land of Israel, was desolated long ago, first, by Nebuchadnezzar, and the second time by Alexander the Macedonian."* This one plain and undeniable fact completely overthrows R. Isaac's premises, and shows that the prophecy begins its fulfilment at the time of Alexander the Great, i. e., in the time of the second temple, and thence stretches forward to the times of the Messiah. It fixes the chronology with certainty down to the seventh verse, for the fall of the Philistines is by the prophet

* והנה צור שהיתה סמוכה לארץ ישראל כבר נחרבה זה ימים רבים והיתה חרבנה שתי פעמים אחת ע"י נבוחד נאצר ושנית ע"י אלכסנדרוס מוקדון ·

intimately connected with the destruction of Tyre. After the prediction of this event, he adds, "Ashkelon shall see it, and fear," &c. But if the first seven verses refer to the time of Alexander, why should not the eighth verse, which is closely connected with the former, and which, according to Aben Ezra,* concludes a paragraph? This verse says, "I will encamp about mine house because of the army, because of him that passeth by, and because of him that returneth;" and there is a circumstance in the history of this period, which seems exactly to fulfil it, that is, Alexander's treatment of the Jewish high-priest, and the preservation of the temple. There is one difficulty not urged by R. Isaac, but which must be considered. The prophet adds, "And no oppressor shall pass through them any more; for now I have seen with mine eyes;" whereas, after this, the Jews suffered much from the Gentiles, and were finally driven forth from their land, and the temple itself was destroyed. From this, Jews and Christians, too, may argue, that the third temple, and not the second, is intended; but this will not prove that Jesus is not the Messiah, or that he was not to appear in the second temple. For, if the third temple be intended, the prophet evidently departs from the chronological order, and makes a sudden transition from the time of Alexander, when Tyre and Philistia were destroyed, to the last days and to events which must, in every case, be posterior to the coming of the Messiah. The only question, then, can be, as to how long posterior? But this the prophet does not decide. If the prophet had said, that this state of security was to be cotemporaneous with the coming of Messiah, or to take place within a very few years after his advent, it might be argued, that as this was not ful-

* Aben Ezra begins his Commentary on the ninth verse by saying, "This is the beginning of a paragraph."

filled in the appearance of Jesus, he is not the Messiah. But the prophet does not define any time, he simply states, that there was to be such a state of things. It can, therefore, be no argument against the claims of our Lord. If it be urged, that the Messiah is mentioned in the next verse, and that 1700 years have already rolled away, and that this is too long a period to suppose between the eighth and ninth verses, we reply, that if the prophet speaks of the third temple in the eighth verse, there is a much longer period between the subjects of the seventh and eighth verses, for in the former he was speaking of the time of Alexander, since when two thousand years have passed away, and we do not see the third temple yet.

Admitting, then, the strongest case that the Jews can make out, it will not affect the proof of our Lord's Messiahship; but still, from the nature of the preceding context, all referring to the times of the second temple, I am inclined to believe that the eighth verse refers to the second temple also, and that the difficulty arising from the words, "No oppressor shall pass through them any more," is to be solved by considering this promise as of the same nature as most of the others made to Israel, that is, conditional upon their obedience. Moses has repeatedly laid down this as the general principle of God's dealings with the Jews, especially in reference to the possession of blessing and prosperity in the land. As for example, "See, I have set before thee this day life and good, and death and evil: in that I command thee this day to love the Lord thy God, to walk in his ways, and to keep his commandments, and his statutes, and his judgments, that thou mayest live and multiply: and the Lord thy God shall bless thee in the land whither thou goest to possess it. But if thine heart turn away, so that thou wilt not hear, but shalt be drawn away, and worship other gods and serve them; I denounce unto you this day, that ye shall surely perish, and that ye shall not prolong your days upon the land whither thou passest over Jordan to possess it." (Deut. xxx. 15—18.) There are similar passages, almost without number, in which the blessings are suspended upon the condition of obedience, so that this may fairly be considered as the fundamental principle, according to which the other similar promises are to be explained. If not, then the Mosaic law must be considered as absolutely abolished, and it must be admitted that a new principle has been introduced, which no Jew can concede, nor any Christian either. For, though we believe, that, as a religious dispensation for the Church of God, the Mosaic law has been entirely abrogated, yet we believe that, because the Jews did not receive the Prophet like unto Moses, God has required it of them and dispersed them; that is, we believe that the denunciations of the Mosaic law against the nation are still in force, and are now actually fulfilling; and, if so, then the Mosaic principle of obedience or disobedience as the condition of national weal or woe is still in force, and consequently by that fundamental principle, every promise to the Jews must be tried and interpreted, no matter whether the condition is expressed or not. The law of Moses is the great foundation upon which all the national promises rest.

The necessity and truth of this principle may be tried by applying it to the particular promises, even those made before the time of Moses. God said to Abraham, "I will give unto thee, and to thy seed after thee, the land wherein thou art a stranger, all the land of Canaan for an everlasting possession." But Israel has never yet enjoyed the benefit of that promise. Has the Word of God failed then? No; God gave it to them, but they did not fulfil the conditions of tenure. It is still theirs, just as a sequestrated estate belongs to the lawful heir, although he does not enjoy the possession until the condition of paying just debts, on which all estates are enjoyed, has been fulfilled. God has not taken away the right of possession and given it to another. That still belongs to the Jews, and whenever they fulfil the conditions, they shall again have the actual enjoyment of the inheritance. Again, when God sent Moses to the Israelites, he gave him this promise, "I will bring you in unto the land, concerning the which I did swear to give it to Abraham, to Isaac, and to Jacob; and I will give it you for an heritage: I am the Lord." (Exod. vi. 8.) This is a very solemn promise, and apparently unconditional. But it was not fulfilled to those to whom it was made. Instead of entering into the land, they all, with few exceptions, died in the wilderness. Why, then, was it not fulfilled to them, and why was it fulfilled to their children? Because the condition of obedience was implied which they did not fulfil, but their children did.

It would be very easy to multiply similar passages from Moses and the other prophets, but I shall content myself with one other instance, taken from Zechariah himself, and couched in terms very similar to the passage under consideration. In the second chapter we find the following words, "Jerusalem shall be inhabited as towns without walls, for the multitude of men and cattle therein. For I, saith the Lord, will be unto her a wall of fire round about, and will be the glory in the midst of her. Ho, ho, Come forth; and flee from the land of the north, saith the Lord; for I have spread you abroad as the four winds of the heaven, saith the Lord. Deliver thyself, O Zion, that dwellest with the daughter of Zion." (Zech. ii. 4, &c.) Here is a magnificent promise made to those who should return from Babylon, but it has never yet been fulfilled. Jerusalem, rebuilt by the exiles, never was inhabited thus, nor did the Lord give the miraculous protection here promised. Are we then to conclude that the Lord broke his promise? No such thing, the original terms of Israel's national contract or covenant presuppose a condition here and in all similar promises; that condition was not fulfilled by the Jews, and therefore the promised blessings were withheld. But, whenever Israel fulfils the condition, the Lord will accomplish his promise to the letter.

A Jew may attempt to turn this principle against Christianity. He may say, Then the promise of the coming of Messiah was also conditional upon obedience, but the Jews have been disobedient, and, therefore, Messiah is not come. But this admits of an easy answer. The promise of a Messiah was not a merely national promise, it was made to all mankind, and therefore the disobedience of the Jews could not prevent what God had promised to the other nations. But the national blessings promised to the Jews at his coming were conditional, and as they have not fulfilled the conditions, those blessings have been withheld. And thus we have an answer to R. Isaac's next objection. He explains the words, "I will cut off the chariot from Ephraim, and the horse from Jerusalem," to mean, that Israel shall no more have need of weapons of war, because there shall be universal peace. Israel did not choose to receive the Messiah when he came; it was, therefore, utterly impossible that God could bestow the blessings. R. Isaac's next objection is founded on a false interpretation of the words, "He shall speak peace to the heathen." He says, "This means, that the King Messiah will make peace between nation and nation, if there be wars between them, for all the heathen shall obey him."* Now, though we believe, on the authority of other prophecies, that a time shall yet come, when there shall be universal peace, we must deny that it is promised in these words. It is not said, that he will *make* peace between the heathen, but that "he will *speak* peace

* It is odd enough that Hengstenberg should adopt this interpretation.

to the heathen." There is one other passage where this expression occurs. It is said of Mordecai, "He was accepted of the multitude of his brethren, seeking the wealth of his people, and speaking peace to all his seed, וְדֹבֵר שָׁלוֹם לְכָל־זַרְעוֹ." (Esth. x. 3.) Here the parallelism is against R. Isaac's intepretation; but I will give Aben Ezra's commentary to show how a Jew would understand the words in a passage having no relation to controversy. He says, "*Seeking the wealth of his people.* It would have been enough for him to have done good to those that sought it of him, but behold he was himself seeking to do good to his people. 'His seed.' These are his sons, and his son's sons, and sons are always afraid of their fathers. But he was in the habit of speaking peace at first even to his sons, who were as his servants, and still more to his people. This verse shows his high moral attainments and his meekness, as it is recorded of Moses, our master, that he was a meek man above all men." (Aben Ezra in loc.) This shows, then, that Aben Ezra considered this expression to mean, not that he would make peace between his seed, but that, in all humility and meekness, he should speak words of peace to them. And this meaning can easily be confirmed by the general usage of the language. In the first place, when דִּבֶּר is construed with an accusative, it is generally the accusative of the thing spoken; as דִּבֶּר הָאִישׁ אֲדֹנֵי הָאָרֶץ אִתָּנוּ קָשׁוֹת, "The man, the lord of the land, spake roughnesses with us." (Gen. xlii. 30.) דַּבְּרוּ אֱמֶת, "Speak the truth." (Zech. viii. 16.) שֶׁקֶר דִּבַּרְתָּ, "Thou hast spoken falsehood." (Zech. xiii. 3.) So that, following the idiom of the language, "He shall speak peace," would naturally mean, He shall speak words of peace. But, besides, it is to be observed, that here it is followed by a dative, and that in such cases the dative always signifies the person spoken to, as may be seen on almost every page of the Hebrew Bible; and דִּבֶּר then often signifies to announce, or promise; as, of the blessings which Jacob announced to his sons, it is said, "This is it that their father spake unto them, דִּבֶּר לָהֶם. The Lord God of your fathers make you a thousand times so many more as ye are, and bless you, as he hath promised you, דִּבֶּר לָכֶם." (Deut. i. 11.) "Prophesy unto us smooth things, דַּבְּרוּ לָנוּ חֲלָקוֹת." (Isaiah xxx. 10.) The usage of the language therefore determines, that there is no ground whatever for R. Isaac's interpretation, but that the true meaning of "He shall speak peace to the heathen," is, "He shall promise or announce peace to the heathen," which sense will confirm, not weaken, the claims of Jesus of Nazareth.

In connexion with this passage he makes another objection; he says, "Of the King Messiah it is said, 'He shall speak peace to the Gentiles.' But Jesus, the Nazarene, says, I am not come to send peace, but a sword.' It is easy to show that these passages do not contradict one another, but the best answer is an appeal to facts. Did Christ speak peace to the Gentiles, and has his prediction of the arising of strife been fulfilled? If both things have really happened, which it is easy to show, then the event shows that there is no contradiction, and that, more satisfactorily than any argument.

One answer will suffice for his remaining objections, which are, I. In the days of the Messiah both Judah and Ephraim are to be gathered. II. That many nations shall be joined to the Lord. III. That Gog and Magog shall come up against Israel, and fall before the children of Judah and Ephraim. IV. That there shall be peace in all the world. V. That King Messiah's dominion shall extend over the whole earth. The fourth objection has been answered already. The second is answered by the conversion of the Gentiles from idolatry. And to the other three it is enough to reply, that the prophet does not promise that all these things are to happen as soon as the Messiah comes. The days of Messiah are to last from his coming to the end of the world, but the prophet does not mark out the period of this great interval, in which these events are to take place. On the contrary, arguing only from this prophecy, without a reference to others, we may infer, that Messiah's glory was not to commence with his coming. For the prophet describes him as "a lowly, afflicted man, and riding on an ass," which tells us plainly that his beginning is to be in humiliation, not in glory. And, further, the prophet gives a very significant intimation, that the deliverance of Israel was to be posterior to the spread of his dominion amongst the Gentiles; for, after the prediction that he should speak peace to the Gentiles, and that his dominion should be from sea to sea, he adds, most significantly, "As for thee also, by the blood of thy covenant I have sent forth thy prisoners out of the pit wherein is no water," which the Jewish commentators interpret of the deliverance of the Jews: now, if this deliverance was to take place immediately on the coming of the Messiah, why should he, as it were, make it a secondary event, and connect it with the preceding passage by an "also?" The very form of the address, "As for thee also," intimates that there should be something wrong with Israel, but that, notwithstanding, they should be ultimately delivered.

Having thus answered the objections, I will now briefly show that the circumstances of our Lord's advent do answer to the prediction.

I. The time of his advent. The prophet here connects the coming of Messiah with the times of the second temple, and after the destruction of Damascus, Tyre, and Philistia, by the Greeks. At this time Jesus of Nazareth appeared.

II. The circumstances of his advent. He was just or righteous, so that none of his judges found any fault in him, and he himself could challenge the Jews to convince him of sin. He was saved by the Lord from all his enemies, and rose triumphantly from the dead. He was lowly and afflicted, and he did literally ride into Jerusalem upon an ass.

III. The results of his coming. He spoke peace to the Gentiles, and his dominion does even now extend to the ends of the earth. Within three centuries from his appearance, Christianity held the sceptre of the world. And though Mahometanism offered a temporary obstacle to its extension, we now see that power prostrated, and Christianity holding within its grasp the means of universal empire. From India to America; from the extreme north, down to the newly-discovered islands of the Southern Ocean, Christianity possesses the ascendancy, and Christians, if not restrained by those principles of love, justice, and holiness, which Jesus has taught them, might, at any moment, take possession of the world. It is true, we, as well as the Jews, look for something far beyond this, but that which we see with our eyes, is a pledge that God will accomplish the remainder. Never since the beginning of the world did any form of religion possess such power, or extend so widely as the religion of Jesus. The most powerful, the most civilised, the most scientific nations that the world ever saw, acknowledge Jesus as their Lord, and the sun never sets upon his kingdom.

IV. Whilst his dominion has been spreading amongst the Gentiles, the Jews still remain in the pit where there is no water, as the prophet intimates, and God still cries to them, Turn to the strong-hold, ye prisoners of hope; and I will cause the Messiah to return to you.

CHAPTER X.

1. " *Ask ye.*"—In that time, if ye ask of God, blessed be He, rain in the time of the latter rain, the Lord who makes the lightnings will immediately hear your prayer, and make lightnings,* and will give rain. The lightnings shall be with the rain, as it is said, וְדֶרֶךְ לַחֲזִיז קֹלוֹת, " And a way for the lightnings of the thunder."† These are they which flash in the time of rain before the crash comes. The root of this word is חָזָה. Our rabbies, of blessed memory, have interpreted it to mean cloud. As to that which is said, " In the time of the latter rain," which is the last rain, and falls in the days of Nisan, the meaning is, Yea, even at the last, if they want rain, he will give it them, and the herb shall grow quickly.

מְטַר גֶּשֶׁם (rain of rain). Two synonymes are here put together in regimen, as אַדְמַת עָפָר, " earth of dust" (Dan. xii. 2), and מִטִּיט הַיָּוֵן, " out of the miry clay" (Ps. xl. 3), to signify abundance of rain, which he will give to those who live in that time.

" *To every one grass in the field.*"—To every one of them he will give grass in the field. Our rabbies, of blessed memory, have interpreted it thus: " In the time when Israel doeth the will of God, He doeth their will: so that if one man alone, and not the others, want rain, he will give rain to that one man, and if a man want one herb alone in his field or garden, and not another, he will give rain to that one herb, according as one of the saints

* Bright clouds; compare margin.

† Though Kimchi only quotes the last half of this verse, his allusion is really to the whole. " When he made a decree for the rain," &c. (Job xxviii. 24.)

used to say, This plot of ground wants rain, and that plot of ground does not want rain, [and so the rain fell.] *

2. "*For the Teraphim have spoken vanity.*"—Then they shall know that the Teraphim have spoken vanity, for they shall see that the prophecies uttered by the true prophets are fulfilled. The evil prophecies have been fulfilled in the desolation of the land, and the consolations shall be fulfilled at that time. Then they shall know that the possessors of Teraphim who led them astray before the desolation of the land, and also the diviners and the false prophets with their dreams, who, before the desolation, used to promise them peace, then they shall know that they gave vain comfort, and that all was lie, and vanity, and nothingness.

"*Therefore they went their way as a flock.*"—They went their way, and were led in captivity from their land, as a flock that has no shepherd.

"*They were abased (English, troubled) because there was no shepherd.*"—יַעֲנוּ means, "They were humbled;" as וּמֵהֲמוֹנָם לֹא יַעֲנֶה, "Nor abase himself for the noise of them" (Isa. xxxi. 4), where also this root has the meaning of humbling.†

3. "*Against the shepherds.*"—These are the kings of Greece, who oppressed Israel before the day when the house of the Hasmoneans rose up against them. After likening Israel to a flock, he likens the kings that ruled to shepherds, or he-goats that go before the flock, and the flock after them.

"*Upon the he-goats I will visit.*"—Their sin upon them.

"*For the Lord of hosts hath visited.*"—He hath remembered their affliction and oppression, and hath promised to save them.

* Talm. Bab. Taanith, fol. ix., col. 2.

† And so our translators have in that passage.

"*His flock.*"—He will not leave them in the hand of the shepherds any longer.

"*And hath made them as his goodly horse in the battle.*"—As a horse whose strength and might are seen in the battle, as it is said of him, "He rejoices in his strength: he goeth on to meet the armed men." (Job xxxix. 21.)

4. "*Out of him is the corner.*"—Corner is spoken parabolically of the head of the people, as it is said, "Draw ye near hither all the corners of the people" (1 Sam. xiv. 38), i. e., the heads of the people. The meaning here in Zechariah is, that the head over them shall not be from the Greeks.

"*The nail.*"—This is the governor; and so it is said, "I will fasten him as a nail in a sure place." (Isaiah xxii. 23.)

"*The battle bow.*"—For they shall not want the help of another people: their hands alone shall be sufficient for them.

"*Out of him came forth every oppressor together.*"—For they shall oppress their enemies.

5. "*And they shall be as mighty men which tread down in the mire of the streets.*"—Israel shall be as the mighty men of Greece, such as they were at first, and they shall be treading and trampling their enemies in the mire of the streets.

"*In the battle (war).*"—In that war which they shall wage with them.

"*And the riders on horses shall be ashamed.*"—The enemies who came against them riding on horses shall have shame, for Israel shall overcome them, though on foot.

6. "*And I will strengthen.*"—I will give them strength against their enemies.

"*And I will bring them again.*"—וְהוֹשְׁבוֹתִים is a word compounded of וְהוֹשַׁבְתִּים, "And I will cause them to dwell," from ישב; and of וְהֹשְׁבוֹתִים (And I will cause them to return), from שׁוּב; and the two ideas are here both implied, that is to say, He will cause them to return to their land, and will cause them to dwell there in peace and security.

"*And they shall be as though I had not cast them off.*"—They shall be in great honour and in peace, as if I had never cast them off, for on account of the abundance of good they will not remember their afflictions which are past.

7. "*And Ephraim, they shall be like a mighty man.*"—They shall all be in the war as a mighty man, as has been said above, "They shall be as mighty men."

"*Their heart shall rejoice.*"*—Their heart shall rejoice when they overcome their enemies.

"*As wine.*"—As one that drinketh wine, as Jonathan also has interpreted it, "As they that drink wine." A similar ellipse occurs in חֲמוּדוֹת אָתָּה, "Thou art desires" (Dan. ix. 23), i.e., A man of desires. And again: "Wine is a mocker;" i.e., He that drinketh wine. And there are many other similar passages.

"*Their children shall see and rejoice.*"—The little ones and the youths, who are not accustomed to make war, shall see the war of their fathers, and when they overcome their enemies they shall rejoice.

8. "*I will hiss for them.*"—שרק signifies the moving of the lips with the voice, and it is a sign of calling, as "He will hiss unto them from the end of the earth." The meaning of the word is, "*I will gather them.*" Some commentators refer this to the fact, that they had been dispersed by reason of the persecutions by the Greek kings, but in the days of the Hasmonean house had returned to the

* Here in English it would seem as if Kimchi only repeated the words of Scripture. But in the Hebrew the sense is expressed by a perfect with Vau conversive, and Kimchi gives the future.

land of Israel. Other commentators refer this verse to the future.

"*And they shall increase as they increased.*"—As they increased in the land of Egypt, so shall they increase at that time.

9. "*And I will sow them among the peoples.*"—Some commentators refer this to the time when they were scattered amongst the nations on account of the persecutions by the Greek kings, but there they remembered God and his commandments.

"*And they shall live with their children and turn again,*" to their land, in the days of the Hasmoneans. But others say, "I will sow them among the peoples" means, After their salvation, in the days of the Hasmoneans, they shall go amongst the Gentiles, to trade or make an excursion, and shall be greatly honoured amongst them, on account of the salvation which God, blessed be He, wrought for them.

"*And they shall live with their children and turn again.*"—When they shall return to their land, they shall return with great wealth, wherewith they shall live with their children.

10. "*I will bring them again from the land of Egypt, and from Assyria.*"—They had gone forth thence on account of the afflictions.

"*To the land of Gilead and Lebanon.*"—Gilead is beyond the Jordán eastward; and Lebanon includes all the land of Israel on this side, as it is said, "That goodly mountain, and Lebanon." (Deut. iii. 25.)

"*And there shall not be found for them.*"—It will not be sufficient for them, on account of their multitude. But Jonathan has interpreted "Lebanon and the Sanctuary" as Onkelos has also done.

11. "*And he shall pass through the sea, affliction.*"—As to the nations, who are many like the sea, affliction

shall pass through them. The verb is masculine, i. e., to say, "the matter of affliction." *

"*And shall smite the waves in the sea.*"—God, blessed be He, will smite in the sea and on its waves, and will dry them up, that is to say, the multitude of the nations; and this is what is said, "And all the depths of the river shall dry up," as is explained, "The pride of Assyria shall be brought down." Assyria and Egypt are mentioned because they did more evil to Israel than the other nations.

12. "*And I will strengthen them in the Lord.*"—Similar to, "And he said unto Moses, Come up unto the Lord." (Exod. xxiv. 1.)†

Behold we have expounded this chapter, according to the opinion of the commentators, of the second temple: but my own decided opinion is, that it is entirely future, as well as that which preceded. And this is proved by the mention of Judah and Ephraim, for in the days of Messiah all Israel shall return to their land, both Judah and Ephraim, who did not return in the second temple, but only the captives of Babylon, who were Judah and Benjamin. Whenever Judah is mentioned, Benjamin is included, for Benjamin was joined with Judah. And the mention of Greece (Javan) includes Gog and Magog, for they were brothers, of the sons of Japhet; and all shall come in the days of the Messiah. Jonathan has interpreted, "against thy sons, O Greece," against the sons of the nations, as we have written. The whole chapter is plain, according to this interpretation. And as to that which is said, "I will sow them amongst

* צָרָה is feminine, and therefore cannot agree with the verb וְעָבַר, which is masculine. The parallelism shows that our translators have given the true sense.

† Here, again, plurality of persons in the Deity is plainly intimated.

the Gentiles," the meaning is, according to the opinion of the Targumist, as we have written. Also the meaning of "He shall pass through the sea, affliction," is as I have given it, or it may be taken literally, as is said in Isaiah, "The Lord shall smite the tongue of the Egyptian sea," &c.

CHAPTER XI.

1. " *Open thy doors, O Lebanon.*"—The commentators have explained this of the overthrow of the Hasmonean dynasty, or of the time of the desolation of the second temple. But it is more consistent to interpret it in connexion with the subject immediately preceding, of the destruction of the kings of the nations. This was the opinion of Jonathan, who has rendered the words " Ye nations, open your gates."

2. " *Howl, fir-tree.*" —Jonathan says, " Howl, ye kings."

" *Defenced forest.*"—בָּצִיר must be interpreted as עָרִים בְּצֻרוֹת, " fenced cities." (2 Kings xix. 25.) הַבָּצוּר is written with ו, but is read with Yod, but the meaning is the same. However בָּצִיר may be also interpreted " vintage," as וְהִשִּׂיג לָכֶם דַּיִשׁ אֶת־בָּצִיר, " And your threshing shall reach unto the vintage." (Lev. xxvi. 5.) They are compared to trees of the forest, and are put in connexion with " the vintage," because they were bearing fruit, i. e., they were rich and great, possessors of goods, and cattle, and property.

3. " *The howling of the shepherds —— their glory.*"—Their strength, and might, and their glory. The interpretation of the verse is according to the Targum.* But our rabbies, of blessed memory, have interpreted this chapter of the desolation of the second temple, and Lebanon is the holy temple. They say, that forty years before the destruction of the temple, the doors of the sanctuary opened of themselves. Rabban Johanan ben Zakkai reproved them, and said, " O sanctuary, sanc-

* The Targum says, " The voice of the crying of the kings, because their provinces are desolated."

tuary! how long wilt thou terrify thyself? I know that thine end is to be left desolate, for Zechariah has prophesied against thee long since, 'Open thy doors, O Lebanon.'" *

4. "*Thus saith the Lord; Feed the flock of the slaughter.*"—Most interpreters explain this paragraph of the past: that he told the prophet to prophesy what should happen to Israel until their captivity. Some interpret it of the second temple. They are called "the flock of the slaughter" because they were given into the hands of their enemies to be slain, when they transgressed the commands of the blessed God. My Lord, my father, of blessed memory, has explained רְעֵה, "feed," as an infinitive, "to feed," and gives as an example of a similar form, לְמַעַן הֱיֵה־לָּה בָּרָק, "that there may be to it a glittering" (Ezek. xxi. 10, Heb. 15), where הֱיֵה has the same signification as לִהְיוֹת. The meaning then is,

* The remarkable tradition which Kimchi here quotes, is found in the Talm. Bab. Treatise. Yoma. fol. 39, col. 2, and is as follows:—"Our rabbies have handed down the tradition, that forty years before the destruction of the temple, the lot [*for the goat that was to be sacrificed on the day of atonement*] did not come out on the right side—neither did the scarlet tongue [*that used to be fastened between the horns of the scape-goat*] turn white [*as, according to tradition, it used to do, to signify that the sins of the people were forgiven*]—neither did the western lamp burn—the doors of the sanctuary also opened of their own accord, until R. Johanan, the son of Zakkai, reproved them. He said, O sanctuary, sanctuary! why dost thou trouble thyself? I know of thee that thine end is to be left desolate, for Zechariah, the son of Iddo, has prophesied against thee long since, 'Open thy doors, O Lebanon, that the fire may devour thy cedars.' R. Isaac, the son of Tavlai, says, Why is the temple called Lebanon [white mountain]? Answer: Because it makes white the sins of Israel. Rav Zutra, the son of Tobiah, says, Why is temple called 'forest' (Zech. xi. 2)? Answer: Because it is written, 'The house of the forest of Lebanon' (1 Kings vii. 2), &c." Lightfoot, on Matt. xxvi. 3, quotes this tradition from the Jerusalem Talmud in nearly the same words; and, on John x. 1, gives his view of this xith chapter of Zechariah, which is worth consulting.

"The Lord said, to feed the flock," but not that he commanded the prophet to feed them himself. God, blessed be He, said to feed them, as he says in verse 7, "And I will feed the flock of the slaughter."

5. "*Whose buyers slay them.*"—And behold they are in the hands of a buyer and seller, who has no mercy.

"*And they are not guilty.*"—They do not hold themselves guilty if they kill them.

"*They that sell them.*"—וּמֹכְרֵיהֶן יֹאמַר. [The plural noun and singular verb signify] that each one of their sellers says, when he sells them, Blessed be the Lord.

"*For I am rich.*"—Blessed be the Lord, for I am rich from the price of these captives. And when the wicked seller says, Blessed be the Lord, it is because he thinks that God is well pleased with the deed, as Sennacherib said, "Am I now come up without the Lord against this land to destroy it?" (Isa. xxxvi. 10) or, it is said because it is the custom of the children of men in this world to thank God for every increase of their gain, whether it be gotten in the way of righteousness or unrighteousness. And on this subject our rabbies, of blessed memory, say, "A thief, when he is in the act of breaking in, calls upon God."

וָאעְשִׁר. The א is quiescent, the ו has pathach, and the ע only a simple sh'va.

"*And their own shepherds pitieth them not.*"—And God, for he is their own shepherd,* has no pity upon them; and therefore they fell into the hands of their enemies, who buy and sell them. רֹעֵיהֶם, *shepherds*, is said in the plural number, similar to the idiom in יִשְׂמַח יִשְׂרָאֵל בְּעֹשָׂיו, "Let Israel rejoice in his makers." (Ps. cxlix. 2.) And again, אַיֵּה אֱלוֹהַּ עֹשָׂי, "Where is God my makers." (Job xxxv. 10.)

* This is a remarkable exposition, as furnishing another instance of the plural being applied to God.

6. "*For I will no more pity them,*" unless they better their doings.

"*Upon the inhabitants of the land*" of Israel.

"*Every one into his neighbour's hand, and into the hand of his king.*"—They shall destroy them: and their king, he also shall destroy them, whether it be a king of Israel, or a king of the Gentiles, that ruleth over them. מַמְצִיא has the signification of מַזְמִין, "deliver into," &c., as הָעוֹלָה הִמְצִיאוּ אֵלָיו לִנְתָחֶיהָ, "And they presented the burnt-offering unto him, with the pieces thereof." (Lev. ix. 13.)

"*And they shall smite the land.*"—Between the one and the other they shall destroy and waste the land of Israel.

"*And out of their hand will I not deliver them,*" because they have sinned against me.

7. "*And I will feed truly the poor of the flock,*" לָכֵן.—In truth the poor of the flock I found them, when I took them to feed. First, I will explain this paragraph according to the opinion of those commentators who refer it to the past; and although I do not find that any one of them has given a complete commentary, I will explain according as I shall find in my opinion, by the help of the Name, blessed be He.

"*And I took unto me two staves.*"—It is the way of a shepherd to lead the flock with the staff in his hand; but it is said that to feed Israel he took two staves, this is to signify that his mode of leading them was not uniform, but according to their deeds so he led them, and, therefore, two staves are mentioned. And it is said, "The one I called Beauty, and the other Bands." לְאַחַד is here twice pointed with pathach, though it is not in regimen. This is not according to the prevailing custom, but some few similar cases are found. It is said, that he called one of the staves "Beauty," for in pleasantness he led them on the way: as David, the king, says, "The Lord is my shepherd, I shall not want. He maketh me to lie down in green pastures; he leadeth me beside the still waters." This was in the time when Israel kept the way of the Lord, when their kings and their judges were good, and leading them in the right way, and then God led them in pleasantness, full of all goodness, without any adversary or evil occurrence.

"*And the other*" of the staves he called "Bands" (Destroyers). חֹבְלִים is the language of destruction, as מְחַבְּלִים כְּרָמִים, "That spoil the vines (Song ii. 15); that is to say, they have corrupted their way and their doings, and he led them accordingly, in that he was not careful to preserve them from their enemies. Nevertheless he still led them, so that his Shechinah and his protection did not depart from them until their captivity, for there were good kings and bad kings after them. When they were evil, then evil came upon them, and then the staff (Destroyers) was there; but when they did good, then the good came upon them, and the staff, Beauty (pleasantness), was there.

"*And I fed the flock.*"—Whether good or evil, I fed them.

8. "*Three shepherds also I cut off in one month.*"—These are the sons of Josiah, Jehoahaz, and Jehoiakim, and Zedekiah; these three died by the hand of their enemies. But Jehoiakin, the son of Jehoiakim, although he was led away captive was not cut off, for from him the kingdom, the kingdom of the house of David was continued, but these three were cut off, for from the seed of Jehoahaz and Zedekiah there was no king: and Jehoiakin died in dishonour, torn and cast out; and these three were at the end of the desolation and captivity of the land, for the three together did not reign more than twenty-two years and four months, and they were all in affliction. The words, "In one month," signify a short time, as in Hosea v. 7, "Now shall a month devour them and their portions."

"*And my soul was straitened,*" וַתִּקְצַר נַפְשִׁי. This is said figuratively, as in Judges x, 16, וַתִּקְצַר נַפְשׁוֹ בַּעֲמַל יִשְׂרָאֵל, "And his soul was shortened for the misery of Israel." The same idea is intended as that expressed by Ezekiel, in the words—

וַתֵּקַע נַפְשִׁי מֵעָלֶיהָ כַּאֲשֶׁר נָקְעָה נַפְשִׁי מֵעַל אֲחוֹתָהּ.

"Then my soul was alienated from her, like as my soul was alienated from her sister." (Ezek. xxiii. 18.) These two verses refer to the desolation of the land in the days of Zedekiah. And when it is said, "Their soul also abhorred me," the meaning is, My soul did not loathe them first, but their soul first despised me, therefore my soul abhorred them. But Jonathan has not thus interpreted the verse, "His soul was shortened for the misery of Israel," and he has interpreted, "My soul was shortened for them," to mean, "My word has removed them;" and again, the words, "Their soul also abhorred me," he has interpreted, "Because their soul abhorred my service." And again the words, "Three shepherds I cut off," &c., he has not expounded the thing, but given the simple meaning of the words, "And I cast away three *governors* in one month."

9. "*Then said I, I will not feed you.*"—Before the temple was desolated, in the days of these three shepherds, when I saw that their deeds were evil, and that no good king would arise after them, I said, I will not feed them any more; in the same way as it is said, "I will hide my face from them, and they shall be devoured."

"*That that dieth, let it die,*" by the pestilence.

"*And that that is cut off, let it be cut off,*" by the sword.

"*And let the rest eat every one the flesh of another,*" in the famine.

10. "*And I took.*"—And I had already taken my staff.

"*Beauty.*"—This is Josiah; for after him there was no good king.

" *And I cut it asunder.*"—By the hands of Pharaoh Necho I removed him.

" *To break,*" לְהָפֵיר, with Tsere and Yod, to make it long. —He says, when I saw that no good king would arise after him, I removed him, in order that the nations might rule over Israel. For they did not keep the way of the Lord, except in spite of the king, as it is written; therefore it is said, To destroy my covenant which I had made with all people, as if God had made a covenant with the nations not to do evil to Israel, for they had done them no evil in the days of Josiah. Even Pharaoh Necho sent to him a message, that he should not make war with him.

11. " *And it was broken in that day.*"—That covenant was broken in the day that Josiah died, for the three shepherds ruled over them, and the nations plundered them, and robbed, and slew, and led away captive.

" *And so the poor of the flock that kept me,* הַשֹּׁמְרִים אֹתִי, *knew that it was the word of the Lord.*"—Those righteous persons amongst them who were keeping me, i. e., what I said to them through the prophets. But the people did not hearken, for they did not believe them, only the good amongst them, who were keeping me, i. e., my word, as וְאָבִיו שָׁמַר אֶת־הַדָּבָר, " But his father kept the word," and when the punishments came, they knew that it was the word of the Lord.

12. *And I said unto them.*"—This is the word of the Lord which he said to them through the prophets.

" *Give me my price.*"—Inasmuch as I have fed (or been a shepherd to you) give my price or hire. By hire, is meant repentance and good works.

" *And if not, forbear.*"—Similar to what Ezekiel said, " Whether they hear, or whether they forbear."

" *So they weighed my price, thirty pieces of silver.*"—There were thirty righteous persons amongst them in the days of these three shepherds, and of them we find

Daniel, Hananiah, Mishael, Azariah, Jeremiah, Ezekiel, and Zephaniah. But it is impossible that there should not have been more, even though they are not mentioned, for, behold, it is written, "The dead bodies of thy servants have they given to be meat unto the fowls of the heaven; the flesh of thy saints unto the beast of the earth." (Psalm lxxix. 2.) But Jonathan has interpreted, "If it be right in your eyes, do my will; if not, forbear. And they did my will; the men partly," i. e., some of the men returned in repentance.

13. "*And the Lord said unto me, Cast it unto the potter,*" הַיּוֹצֵר. The prophet says, that God told him to cast this silver to the יוֹצֵר. And some interpret this word as if it were אוֹצָר (treasure), for the Ehevi letters may be interchanged, and the meaning then is, "The keeper of the treasure;" so Jonathan has interpreted by "Treasurer." This comment then signifies, figuratively, that they (the pious persons spoken of in the preceding verse) should unite in the house of the Lord, and be separate from the people that did evil in the eyes of the Lord. The word יוֹצֵר is used to convey an allusion to the Creator, הַיּוֹצֵר יַחַד לִבָּם הַמֵּבִין וגו׳, "He fashioneth their hearts alike, he considereth," &c. (Psalm xxxiii. 15); for he knoweth the good and the evil, He searcheth the heart, and trieth the reins, for there are some who show themselves as good, but are not good.

"*And I took.*"—So it appeared to him in the prophetic vision, that he took the silver and cast it in the house of the Lord to the potter (or treasurer); but this whole matter had happened many years before, for it occurred in the days of the three shepherds, and signifies, in a figure, that the good were united together, and kept separate from the people, and were not seen with them in the streets, and this is what Jeremiah says, "Run ye, to and fro through the streets of Jerusalem—and seek in the broad places thereof—if there be a man that seeketh the truth: and I will pardon it" (Jer. v. 1), as I have explained it in the book of Jeremiah. The words, "goodly price," אֶדֶר הַיְקָר (magnificence of honour), mean, the house of the Lord, according as is said, "I cast it in the house of the Lord." The meaning is [as if it were written] אֶל אֶדֶר הַיְקָר, To the magnificence of honour. The אֶל, which is written, [before הַיּוֹצֵר] stands in the place of two [i. e., it applies to both יוֹצֵר and אֶדֶר]; and the meaning of the words, אֲשֶׁר יָקַרְתִּי מֵעֲלֵיהֶם, "That I was prized at of them" [that I was honourable from upon them] is, I was honoured in myself, and I turned away from them, on account of the evil of their deeds, and so Jonathan has interpreted.*

14. "*Then I cut asunder.*"—This is said of the destruction, when Zedekiah was destroyed, for that was the end of the destroyers and corrupters, the temple was destroyed and Israel led captive.

"*That I might break the brotherhood between Judah and Israel.*"—The brotherhood which existed between Judah and Israel in the service of idols was broken then. When Judah was led captive, there did not remain an idolater in Israel; for Israel, until they were led away captive, did not cease from the service of idols, in all the afflictions that came upon them. But when they were led captive, and saw that the words of the prophets were verified in the desolation of the land, they no more committed idolatry. And Judah also served idols, until they were led captive, but after their captivity, idolatry was annihilated from amongst them. Behold, then, the brotherhood in idolatry which had existed between them, was destroyed; and so Jonathan has interpreted.

Behold, we have interpreted this chapter of the past,

* The Michlal Jophi on the words אֲשֶׁר יָקַרְתִּי, says, כלומר יקרתי בעצמי וסרתי מעליהם כי לא היתי יקר בעיניהם׃, "The words mean, I was honourable, or precious in myself, but I turned away from them, because I was not precious in their eyes."

but the following chapter is, in every case, a prophecy of the future, of the time of the second temple, and we will explain it after that we shall have explained this chapter of the time of the second temple. My lord, my father, has interpreted thus:—

Joseph Kimchi's Interpretation.

God, blessed be He, says, I began to feed the flock, and I took to me two choice staves for the purpose. חוֹבְלִים נוֹעַם, and נוֹעַם—is the high-priest, and חוֹבְלִים—the king. Of the priest it is said, "The priest's lips should retain knowledge;" and again it is said, "Knowledge shall be pleasant, ינעם, to thy soul." הֹבְלִים is the king, because he is like the רַב חוֹבֵל, captain of the sailors in a ship. (Jon. i. 6.) But this flock, although I fed them with these two staves, and kept away from them other shepherds, i. e., the kings of the nations, did not turn to that which is good; and I sent them three prophets to feed them in my place, and they are Haggai, Zechariah, and Malachi; but as their reproof did not profit them, I cut them off, as it is said, "Three shepherds also I cut off in one month." From this we learn, that they died in one month; and after them there was no prophecy in Israel, as our rabbies, of blessed memory, have said, "After the death of Haggai, Zechariah, and Malachi, prophecy departed from Israel." We find also, that the beginning of their prophecy was in one time, in the second year of Darius. It is said, when I cut off these three shepherds, "my soul loathed them, and their soul also abhorred me." בָּחֲלָה signifies "abhorred;" as in that rabbinical saying, פגה בוחל וצמל, An unripe fig, a ripening fig, and a ripe fig. They say, פגה means the days of childhood. בחל is when the daughter is great, and her father abhors her; and the explanation of צמל is יצאת מלאה, when she is adult, and her father despairs of getting her married, on account of her abiding so long in the house.

"*Then I said, I will not feed you* —— *and I took my staff Pleasantness, and cut it asunder.*"—This signifies, that near the captivity they lost the priesthood. "*Give me my price.*" Turn in repentance, and they did turn, but their repentance was not perfect, but only thirty days of the mourning, which they mourned on account of the high-priest who died; this is meant by the thirty pieces of silver. "*Cast it to the potter,*" יוֹצֵר, i. e., to the treasure, as it is explained "to the house of the Lord, to the house of the יוצר."* The meaning is, Write this prophecy, and lay it in the house of the Lord. And there are some who interpret אֶל הַיּוֹצֵר, to the congregation, as יוֹצֵר גֹּבַי, "The former of the grasshopper." ‡ (Amos vii. 1.)

"*The magnificence of the honour wherewith I was honoured from upon them.*"—The majesty of the glory which I removed from them, inasmuch as in the second temple the Shechinah did not rest.

אֲשֶׁר יָקַרְתִּי means, "Which I withheld," as הֹקַר רַגְלְךָ, "Withdraw thy foot." (Prov. xxv. 17.)

"*Then I cut asunder mine other staff,*" הוֹבְלִים, that is, the king, and he is Agrippas, for in his days Titus led them captive.

R. Abraham of Toledo's Exposition.

The wise man, R. Abraham, the Levite, from Toledo, the author of the "Book of Cabbalah," has interpreted this chapter thus:—

"*Feed the flock of the slaughter.*"—This is the

* In verse 13.

† Kimchi on Amos, amongst other interpretations of these words, says, They may signify אסיפת הארבה, "A collection of locusts;" and it is in this sense that Joseph Kimchi here quotes the words.

building of the second temple; and this that is said, "And I took to me two staves, and I called one נֹעַם, and the other, I called חֹבְלִים." נֹעַם, This is the principality of Zerubbabel and Nehemiah, the Tirshatha, for they were of the children of David, and to them the Lord gave the kingdom of Israel a covenant of salt. חֹבְלִים, This is the kingdom of the priests, for they first built the temple on Mount Gerizzim, and intermarried with the Cutheans, and from them came forth a heresy to the world; and at last Hyrcanus, who held the high-priesthood for forty years, turned Sadducean in the end, and slew the priests, he, and Alexander, his son; and such was also the mind of Aristobulus, his son's son.

"*Three shepherds also I cut off in one month.*"—This signifies these three dignities, The principality of the sons of David, and the monarchy of the Hasmoneans, and the monarchy of their servants. He calls the whole duration of the second temple "one month," because it was in his sight as a few days. And this that is said, "I took my staff, נועם, and cut it asunder, that I might break my covenant," &c., this is the death of Zerubbabel and Nehemiah; for the love was interrupted, and the covenant destroyed, which had existed between them and the kings of Persia. And this that is said, "If it be good in your eyes," &c.,—is what he said, when he was feeding them with his second staff, חוֹבְלִים; and it is as if he said, If it be good in your eyes to walk in the ways of the Lord.

"*And they weighed my price, thirty pieces of silver.*"—A symbol of the thirty years, during which the pious kings reigned, and these are they, Mattathias, called Hasmonai, one year; Judas, his son, six years; Jonathan, his son, six years; Simon, his son, eighteen years; together thirty-one years. And if in them there were defective months, they amount to thirty years, during which the faithful kings reigned. And the words, "The Lord said unto me, "Cast it to the יוֹצֵר, to the אֶדֶר הַיְקָר, which I was honoured from upon them," means, This reward is magnificent and precious, and deserves to be amongst the offerings, and a ransom for the souls of the congregation: and he calls them יוֹצֵר, and the meaning of יוצר, is the same as in the passage, וְהִנֵּה יוֹצֵר גֹּבַי, "And behold he formed grasshoppers" (Amos vii. 1); and what follows, "So I cast it in the house of the Lord to the potter," is the same as the former.

"*So I cut asunder my second staff,*" חֹבְלִים.—This is the uprooting of the kingdom of the Hasmoneans in the days of the חֹבְלִים (destroyers), amongst whom were Hyrcanus and Aristobulus, and his sons.

"*To destroy the brotherhood between Judah,*" i. e., *which* was intended to destroy the brotherhood, as it is written, "As for the beauty of his ornament he set it in majesty" [or for pride]. (Ezek. vii. 20.) And the meaning is, "*Which* he set for majesty;"* and "between the חֹבְלִים," means, that they divided Israel into two kingdoms, as Jeroboam, the son of Nebat did, in whose days the kingdom of the house of David was divided, and the brotherhood between Judah and Israel was destroyed.†

15. "*And the Lord said unto me, Take unto thee yet the instruments of a foolish shepherd.*"—These are the servants. [The house of Herod.]

* He thinks that the relative pronoun is to be supplied in both these passages.

† R. Abraham's meaning is not very clear, but receives some light from the exposition of this same passage given in the Chizzuk Emunah. Upon the words, "I cut asunder my second staff," R. Isaac says, "This represents in a figure the uprooting of the kingdom of the priests, for their kingdom was uprooted, when the love and brotherhood between them was destroyed in the days of Hyrcanus and Aristobulus, his brother, for then the children of Judah and Benjamin, and those of the other tribes who adhered to them, were divided into two factions, and this division was the cause of the destruction of the dynasty of the priests." (See Wagenseil's Tela Ignea, part ii. p. 416.)

" *Woe to the idol shepherd that leaveth the flock! The sword shall be upon his arm ——— darkened.*"—This is Agrippas, who brought up Vespasian and Titus against the land of Israel, and the princes of the robbers who committed all the evils.

15. " *And the Lord said unto me, Take thee yet the instruments of a foolish shepherd.*"—The Name, blessed be He, said to Zechariah, that he should take the instruments of a foolish shepherd in the prophetic vision, and this is a sign of a foolish king who should arise in Israel in the time of the second temple, who should do his deeds in folly. The vessel (instrument) of a foolish shepherd, is different from the vessel of another shepherd. The vessel of a shepherd is, for instance, a sack, into which he puts bread to eat, and a cup to drink out of, and such other things as he needs in the wilderness, when he is feeding the sheep. But the vessel of the foolish shepherd is small and diminished, so that his provision falls out, and when he suffers the want of his food, he becomes angry with the flock, and beats, and has not compassion upon them.

אֱוִלִי, " Foolish," has got a paragogic Jod, as אַכְזָרִי. And this is king Herod, who was a servant of the Hasmoneans, and rose against them, and became king, and took a wife of that family, and managed his kingdom in madness, and slew his wife and his sons, and did many evils in Israel. Jonathan has interpreted, " Prophesy against thc stupid governor."

16. " *For, behold ——— the young one.*"—נַּעַר here answers to טָלֶה, a lamb.

" *That that standeth still.*"—That which standeth in its place, so that it cannot go to feed, he will not feed in its place.

" *And tear their claws (hoofs) in pieces.*"—Not enough that he should not do good, but he will do evil to them, for with his staff he will break their hoofs, that they may not be able to walk. Jonathan has interpreted "He will consume the remnant of them."

17. *Woe to the idol shepherd that leaveth the flock.*—רֹעִי the same as רֹעֶה, as it is found in כְּאֹהֶל רֹעִי, Isaiah xxxviii. 12. עֹזְבִי the same as עֹזֵב; the Jod is paragogic. A similar instance is אֹסְרִי לַגֶּפֶן עִירֹה, "Binding his foal unto the vine." (Gen. xlix. 10.) And again, חֹצְבִי מָרוֹם קִבְרוֹ, "He that heweth him out a sepulchre on high." (Isaiah xxii. 16,) &c.

הָאֱלִיל, "*The idol*" (good for nothing), as רֹפְאֵי אֱלִל "physicians of no value." (Job xiii. 4.) אליל is a thing that is of no use, and this shepherd is Herod or Agrippas.

"*The sword upon his arm.*"—Inasmuch as he afterwards says, "His arm shall be clean dried up, and his right eye utterly darkened, sword is not to be taken literally, but for destruction, as the sword destroys. "Arm" is mentioned to signify the destruction of his strength; and "right eye," to signify the destruction of forethought and counsel in his doings. The right eye is the eye of the heart, as R. Abraham Aben Ezra has written; but he has not interpreted this chapter as we have.

OBSERVATIONS ON CHAPTER XI.

Before we proceed to the interpretation of this prophecy, it is necessary, first, to consider two of Kimchi's translations. The first, that of חֹבְלִים in the seventh verse, is not very important with respect to the controversy, but yet must not be passed altogether in silence. Our translators have rendered this word "Bands," and in the margin "Binders." On the other hand, Kimchi and all the Jewish commentators say, that it means "Destroyers," and support this translation by citing מְחַבְּלִים כְּרָמִים, "That spoil the vines." (Song

ii. 15.) In this they are mistaken; our translators have given in the margin the true literal translation, and in the text, the true sense of the word. In the first place, the authority which the rabbies quote is nothing to the purpose. מְחַבְּלִים, which does, indeed, signify "Destroyers," is the Piel, but we cannot infer from that conjugation, that the word has the same sense in the Kal. To establish their translation, it would be necessary to show that חָבַל in the Kal signifies "to destroy," but no instance of this sense can be produced. But, further, this translation is inconsistent with the sense assigned by the prophet. He says, that the consequence of cutting asunder the staff "Bands," was the dissolution of the brotherhood between Israel and Judah. "Then I cut asunder mine other staff, Bands, that I might break the brotherhood between Judah and Israel." This plainly intimates, that this staff had been the means of binding them together, or keeping them united, and with this sense the translation "Destroyers," is altogether at variance.

That our translators are right, appears from what has already been said. If this staff was the means of binding together Judah and Israel, "Bands" or "Binders" is a most appropriate name for it. And, besides, the verb חָבַל has this sense in the Kal, as appears not only from the derivative חֶבֶל, a band, a rope, but from חֹבֵל, the singular of the word under consideration. חֹבֵל is used by Ezekiel and Jonah, to signify a sailor, i. e., a binder of the ship-ropes. The literal translation, therefore, is "Binders." *

* Hengstenberg (whose Commentary on this chapter is one of the noblest specimens of interpretation that I have ever met with, and to which I am largely indebted) takes חֹבְלִים intransitively to signify *Verbundenen*, "Allied or united." But I think that the active signification, "Binders," is more agreeable to the prophet's explanation, which has just been noticed.

The second difference of translation is more important. The words of the thirteenth verse, which our translators have rendered "Cast it unto the potter: a goodly price that I was prized at of them," Kimchi and some other rabbies would have translated thus: "Cast it to the treasure, to the magnificence of honour (i. e., the temple,) in which I was honoured in myself; but I turned away from them." We must show, therefore, that this translation is erroneous, and that the Christian version is correct. In the first place יוֹצֵר, "potter," cannot by any possibility signify "treasure." Kimchi's own words show that he did not believe in this translation. "Some interpret this word as if it were אוֹצָר (treasure), for the Ehevi letters may be interchanged." He does not dare to say, This is the true meaning, but "Some interpret." The reason assigned, namely, that the Ehevi letters may be interchanged, is nothing to the purpose, for this will not account for the difference of punctuation. If the word had been pointed יוֹצָר, there would have been some colour for this interpretation; but the present points show that יוֹצֵר can be nothing else but the present participle of יָצַר, "to form." The rabbies have not even the excuse, that this word occurs but seldom. It is one of the most common words in the language, and never once has any thing like the sense which they here endeavour to force upon it. Indeed this miserable perversion hardly deserves a refutation, for it is given up by some of the most learned of the Jewish commentators. Alshech says that יוֹצֵר is to be taken in its literal sense, "Former," and that it refers to יוצר יתברך, "the blessed Creator." Abarbanel takes it in the same sense, and says, "Cast this matter upon the Lord, for he is the true former and Creator."* And even Kimchi himself says, "The word יוֹצֵר is used to convey an allusion to the Creator," &c.,

* השלך על ה׳ שהו׳ היוצר והבורא האמתי

which is a plain confession that he did not believe it could signify "treasure."

This second translation, however, differs also from the Christian version, and must therefore be considered. It would make the sense to be, "Cast it to the Creator," &c. But to this translation I object; first, because it makes a very harsh transition to the third person, and then back again to the first. It is the Lord that is speaking, and we might therefore expect, if he were speaking of himself, he would not say, "Cast it to the Creator," but, "Cast it to me;" especially as in the following words, אֲשֶׁר יָקַרְתִּי, he speaks of himself in the first person. But, in the second place, the word יוֹצֵר is never used absolutely of the Creator. Whenever it is applied to God, it has either an accusative case or a suffix, as in the example given by Kimchi, הַיּוֹצֵר יַחַד לִבָּם, "He fashioneth their hearts alike." (Ps. xxxiii. 15.) And again: יוֹצֵר עַיִן הֲלֹא יַבִּיט, "He that formed the eye, shall he not see?" (Ps. xciv. 9.) And again: יוֹצֵר אוֹר, "I form the light." (Isa. xlv. 7.) And again, in Zechariah himself: וְיֹצֵר רוּחַ אָדָם, "Which formeth the spirit of man." Often as the word occurs, it is never applied to God absolutely, but always has an accusative; and therefore, as it has no accusative here, I infer that it cannot apply to God, and, therefore, cannot be translated "to the Creator." Having shown that יוֹצֵר cannot signify "treasure" nor "Creator," it follows that the only other translation which it can have, namely, "potter," is the true one: and this may be further seen in Jer. xviii. and xix., where it is universally admitted that הַיּוֹצֵר does mean "potter."

Having been obliged to fix the translation of הַיּוֹצֵר, "the potter," it may be convenient to consider, here, the meaning of the words "Cast it to the potter." They mean the same as "Cast it to an unclean place." The place where the potter worked was in the valley of the son of Hinnom, which had been defiled first by the Moloch-worship of the Israelites, and afterwards by Josiah, who burned human bones there upon the idolatrous altar. This appears from the two chapters of Jeremiah just cited. The Lord says, "Arise, *go down* to the potter's house:" and Jeremiah says, "Then I *went down* to the potter's house" (Jer. xviii. 1—3): from which it appears that the potter's house was situated in the valley beneath the city. But in the following chapter the locality is still more distinctly marked out. "Thus saith the Lord, Go, and get a potter's earthen bottle, בַּקְבֻּק יוֹצֵר חָרֶשׂ, and take of the ancients of the people, and of the ancients of the priests, and go forth to the valley of the son of Hinnom, which is by the entry שַׁעַר הַחַרְסוּת of the *pottery-gate*," not the east-gate, or sun-gate, as our translation has it. That this is the right translation, appears from the play upon the word חָרֶשׂ, "potter's vessel," in the first verse, and which, but for this play, would be quite superfluous, as יוֹצֵר itself signifies "potter," without having חָרֶשׂ appended to it. This play upon words did not escape Rashi, who says, that this gate had its name from the circumstance of their throwing broken earthen vessels there.* The Vulgate also translates "Juxta introitum portæ fictilis." Hence, to cast any thing to the potter was, in fact, to cast it into the valley of the son of Hinnom, and, therefore, signified to cast it into an unclean place, or to reject it with disdain.

I now proceed to the remaining words, which, according to Kimchi, ought to be thus translated: "*To* the magnificence of honour, *in* which I was honoured *in myself, but I turned away* from them." To this translation, if indeed it can be called a translation, I object, because it inserts gratuitously all the words marked in Italics, without the shadow of authority in the Hebrew text. The only word for the insertion of which Kimchi even pretends to account,

* ששם זורקין הרשים הנשברים

is the preposition "to." He says that the preposition אֶל applies both to הַיּוֹצֵר and to אֶדֶר; but this assertion is built on the supposition that הַיּוֹצֵר signifies "The treasure," and that אֶדֶר הַיְקָר (the magnificence of honour) means "the temple;" and that, thus, these two words are in apposition. But we have already proved that the true translation of הַיּוֹצֵר is "the potter," and, therefore, it cannot be in apposition with אֶדֶר; and, therefore, the one preposition אֶל, "to," cannot apply to both words. Indeed, a mere inspection of the accents would determine that אֶדֶר הַיְקָר is not to be connected with הַיּוֹצֵר, but with the following words. The second Sakeph Katon, over הַיְקָר, being nearer the Athnach, has necessarily less power than the first, and shows that this word is to be connected with those that follow. For the insertion of the other words, Kimchi has given no reason, and they must, therefore, be rejected; and when this is done, the translation will not differ much from the Christian interpretation. Stripped of the unauthorised additions, it would stand thus: "Cast it to the potter—the magnificence of honour, which I was honoured from them;" which, in sense, does not differ much from the English version, "a goodly price that I was prized at of them;" and is, owing to the double sense of τιμὴ, almost a literal translation of one of the variants given in Bos's Septuagint, ὑπερμεγέθης ἡ τιμὴ ἣν ἐτιμήθην ὑπ' αὐτων. With this translation we should not quarrel, though we are sure that the English version is more accurate. Kimchi is wrong in rendering יָקַרְתִּי, "I was prized," by נכבדתי, "I was honoured." The meaning of יָקַר is "to be precious, or to be valued," as, for instance, וְיֵיקַר דָּמָם בְּעֵינָיו, "And precious shall their blood be in his sight" (Ps. lxxii. 14); and again וְעַתָּה תִּיקַר נַפְשִׁי בְּעֵינֶיךָ, "Therefore let my life now be precious in thy sight," in both which passages the meaning obviously is, not that the blood or the life of those persons should be honoured, but be valued. And that יקר and נִכבד are not synonymous, appears still more plainly from those words of Isaiah,

מֵאֲשֶׁר יָקַרְתָּ בְעֵינַי נִכְבַּדְתָּ

"Since thou wast precious in my sight, thou hast been honourable." (xliii. 4.) From these and many other passages which might be adduced, it appears that the meaning of יָקַרְתִּי is, I was precious, or valued, or as our translators have given it, "I was prized;" and this determines the meaning of the words אֶדֶר הַיְקָר (connected with it by the accents) to be, Magnificence of price, or value, or, as the English version has it, "goodly price."*

In considering the meaning of the whole passage, the first question is, how are we to understand the command to Zechariah to act the part, first of a good, and then of a foolish shepherd. But this cannot occasion much difficulty or controversy. Zechariah's preceding visions of the four carpenters, the candlestick, the flying roll, &c. &c., lead us at once to the conclusion that this vision is also a symbolical representation, and to this all the commentators, Jewish and Christian, agree. Abarbanel says expressly, what may be inferred from the commentaries of the others, "God commanded him to perform a real action, and in a waking state, which action was to be an intimation and a sign of that which was to happen in God's dealings with Israel;"† and adds,‡ "By attending

* Rosenmüller translates in like manner, Magnificentiam pretii, quo pretiosus habitus sum ab eis. (Scholia in loc.) And Gesenius,—Den herrlichen Preis den ich von ihnen werthgeachtet worden bin, "The glorious price at which I was valued by them." (Lexicon in יָקָר.)

† צוה אותו שיעשה מעשה בפעל ובהקיץ שיהיה הודעה וסימן למה שיהיה בהנהגת ישראל :

‡ ואתה תדע מעניני הנביאים שפעמים היה הק"בה מצוה אליהם שיעשו מעשים בפעל ובהקיץ והיה מבאר להם למה יצוה אותם המעשים כפי הסימן שהיה בהם וכמו שצוה לישעיהו לך ופתחת השק מעל מתניך ונעלך תחלוץ מעל רגלך ויעש כן הלוך ערום ויחף וביאר לו טעם המעשה הזה באומרו כאשר הלך עבדי ישעיהו ערום ויחף שלש שנים אות ומופת על מצרים ועל כוש וגו׳ וכן צוה לו שיקרא את בנו הנולד לו מהר שלל חש בז

to the affairs of the prophets thou mayest know, that God, blessed be He, sometimes commanded them to perform real actions, and in a waking state; and afterwards explained to them the reason of the command according to the sign that was in them. Thus he commanded Isaiah, saying, 'Go, and loose the sackcloth from off thy loins, and put off thy shoe from thy foot. And he did so, walking naked and bare foot' (Isaiah xx. 2); and then explained to him the meaning of this action, saying, 'Like as my servant Isaiah hath walked naked and barefoot, three years, for a sign and wonder upon Egypt and Ethiopia, &c.' In like manner he commanded him to call the name of the son born to him, Maher-shalal-hash-baz, and says, 'For before the child shall have knowledge to cry, My father and my mother, the riches of Damascus and the spoil of Samaria shall be taken away.' (Isaiah viii. 4.) And again, in Jeremiah (xiii. 1, &c.), the hiding of the girdle by the Euphrates, and 'behold, it was marred,' as is there mentioned. In Ezekiel also there are many things of the same kind, real actions performed in a waking state, to which the meaning and explanation are immediately attached, as I have expounded, in the book of Hosea. But sometimes the blessed God commanded the prophets to do things foreign to their character, and unnecessary for them to do, which things were also to be a sign and a type of coming events, and did not expound the meaning, because he knew that

ואמר כי בטרם ידע הנער קרא אבי ואמי ישא את חיל דמשק ואת שלל שמרון וגו׳ וכן בירמיה טמינת האזור בפרת והנה נשחת כמו שנזכר שם וביחזקאל כאלה רבים שהיו דברים נעשים בפעל ובהקיץ וביאורם וטעמם בצדם כמו שפירשתי בספר הושע ופעמים היה ה׳ יתברך מצוה לנביאים שיעשו מעשיהם זרים בחקום או שלא היה בהם צורך להיותם גם׳ כן סימן ורמז למה שיהיה ולא יפרש להם טעם המעשה הוא לפי שידע שיהיה הדבר מובן בעצמו ולא יצטרך אל פירוש · וכזה בישעיהו ויאמר ה׳ אלי קח לך גליון גדול וכתוב עליו בחרט אנוש למהר שלל חש בז ואעידה לי עדים נאמנים וגו׳ ולא ביאר לו השם אז טעם הדבר הזה לפי שהיה ידוע בעצמו וכן ביחזקאל קח לך לבנה וגו׳ וחקות שליע עיר את ירושלם ונתת עליה מצור וגו׳ ולא זכר לו טעם המעשה הזה כי אם מה שאמר בסופו אות היא לבית ישראל וכן קח לך הרב חדה תער הגלבים תקחנה לך והעברת על ראשך ועל זקנך וגו׳ ולא זכר לו ענין המעשה הזה על מה יורה כל אחד מהדברים שצוה בו וגו׳ :

the thing itself could be understood, and did not need an explanation. Thus he said to Isaiah, 'Take thee a great roll, and write in it with a man's pen concerning Maher-shalal-hash-baz. And I took unto me faithful witnesses, &c.' (Isaiah viii. 1, 2), but did not expound the meaning, because it was plain in itself. Thus also in Ezekiel, 'Take thee a tile .... and pourtray upon it the city, even Jerusalem, and lay siege against it, &c.' (Ezekiel iv. 1, 2) where the meaning of this action is not given, excepting that it is said at the end, 'This shall be a sign to the house of Israel.' And again, 'Take thee a sharp knife, take thee a barber's razor, and cause it to pass upon thine head and upon thy beard,' &c. (Ezekiel v. 1), where the subject of the action and the meaning of the details are not mentioned." &c. (Abarbanel Comment. in loc.) Here, though we may not agree with Abarbanel's idea, that this action was performed really and in a waking state, it is evident that he looked upon the vision before us as symbolical, and that this view is fully confirmed by the similar passages in the other prophets, to which he refers.

The next question is, Does this symbolical representation refer to the past, or to the then future, that is, to the times of the first or of the second temple? Here the rabbies are divided. Jonathan, Rashi, and David Kimchi interpret it of the first temple. The two Talmuds, Joseph ben-Gorion,* Aben Ezra, Joseph Kimchi, and Abraham the Levite, Abarbanel, Alshech,† and even R. Isaac, the author of the Chizzuk Emunah,‡ agree with Christians in thinking that it refers to the time of the second temple. Abarbanel refutes the first opinion at great length; his second argument is, however, in itself

* Breithaupt's edition, p. 889.

† The title of Alshech's Commentary on the major and minor prophets is ספר מראות הצובאות.

‡ Part ii. c. 25.

decisive. He asks, "To what purpose should God show the prophet past events, which he had seen with his own eyes, and with the eyes of his father; and what necessity was there to make known to him the captivity of the tribes and the desolation of the first house, which had occurred but a short time before; and [above all] to do this in parables, which are only employed in reference to the future, to make events known before they happen? but with regard to the past, information is not conveyed in parables."* It is not possible to suppose that God would communicate a plain matter of recent history in obscure symbols, and, therefore, the symbolical representation cannot refer to the past, and must predict what was to happen during the time of the second temple. Here, however, there is again a difference of opinion. The Talmud refers the first verses immediately to the time of the destruction of the second temple, the Jewish commentators expound the vision as including the whole time from the restoration from Babylon to the desolation. This latter opinion does not agree with the circumstances pointed out in the text. The whole chapter describes a state of things exactly answering to the condition of the Jews immediately preceding the desolation, but totally different from their state after their return. First, the prophet describes the nation as ready for destruction, and therefore calls them, "The flock of slaughter." Secondly, as forsaken of God, "I will no more pity the inhabitants of the land." Thirdly, as about to be given over to foreign enemies and intestine feuds, "I took my staff, Beauty, and cut it asunder, that I might break my covenant which I had made with all my people." "Then I cut asunder my other staff, even Bands, that I might break the brotherhood between Judah

* למה הראה עתה הק"בה לנביא מה שכבר היה ושהוא ראה בעיניו ובעיני אביו ומה צורך בהודיעו אותו גלות השבטים וחרבן בית ראשון אשר היה זה ימים מעטים ולעשות עליו משלים כי זה לא יעשה כי אם על העתיד להודיעו קודם היותו אבל ממה שכבר עשוהו לא הבוא ההודע׳ במשלים :

and Israel." These particulars show that the symbolical representation refers to the concluding period of the Jewish history.

Having fixed the nature of the prophecy, that it is symbolical, and the time to which it refers, the next question is, What is meant by feeding the flock, and who is intended by the shepherd. The figure of feeding a flock is of frequent occurrence, and is applied to God, and also to the governors and teachers of Israel. Thus Isaiah says, "He shall feed his flock like a shepherd." (xl. 11.) Jeremiah says, "I will give you shepherds according to my heart, which shall feed you with knowledge and understanding." (iii. 15.) And again, "Woe to the shepherds that destroy and scatter the sheep of my pasture." (xxiii. 1.) And in like manner Ezekiel is commanded to prophesy against the shepherds of Israel; "Woe to the shepherds of Israel, that do feed themselves! Should not the shepherds feed the flock?" (Ezekiel xxxiv. 2.) The only difficulty, therefore, that can exist, is in fixing the person intended by the shepherd. Kimchi and the other Jewish commentators affirm that God is the shepherd, and that feeding the flock means his dealings towards the house of Israel. But this, though true to a certain extent, is not an accurate interpretation. The prophet does not speak of God's dealings generally, but of a special attempt to be made for their deliverance, because God himself, in his character of Deity, refuses to feed them any longer. God says to the symbolical shepherd, "Feed the flock of slaughter;" and adds as a reason, "For I will no more pity the inhabitants of the land." The symbolical shepherd cannot, therefore, represent the Deity, for he is commanded to do, what God declares that he will not do. We must therefore inquire, Who is the shepherd elsewhere promised to feed the flock, "whom their own shepherds pity not?" and as soon as we turn to the prophets, we find that the promised shepherd is the Messiah. Jeremiah has a very similar passage to the one we are considering, where, after denouncing woes against the shepherds who scattered the flock, he promises to set up shepherds over them which shall feed them; and then adds, "Behold the days come, saith the Lord, that I will raise unto David a righteous branch" (Jer. xxiii. 1—6); thus pointing out the Messiah as the true shepherd. Ezekiel also, after announcing the judgments to be poured out on the wicked and selfish shepherds, promises the Messiah as the hope of the flock. "I will set up one shepherd over them, and he shall feed them, even my servant David: he shall feed them, and he shall be their shepherd. (xxxxiv. 23.) And again, "David, my servant, shall be king over them: and they all shall have one shepherd" (xxxvii. 24); both of which passages confessedly refer to the Messiah. On the words, "My servant David," Rashi says, מלך מזרעו, "A king from his seed;" and Kimchi says still more expressly,

המשיח שיעמוד מזרעו בעת הישועה׃

"The Messiah, who shall arise from his seed in the time of the salvation." The great similarity that exists between the passage of Zechariah, and those others of Jeremiah and Ezekiel, plainly shows, that they all speak of one person. There is also one feature in the character of the shepherd represented by Zechariah, which is also given elsewhere as a character of the Messiah; and that is, care for the poor. After the command to feed the flock, Zechariah adds, "And so I fed the flock of slaughter, even you, O poor of the flock." * And in the lxxiid Psalm it is predicted of the Messiah, "He shall judge the poor of the people, he shall save the children of the needy."—"He shall spare the poor and needy, and shall save the souls of the needy."

* Our version has the future, "I will feed," but וָאֶרְעֶה ought, certainly, to be translated in the past time.

But one point remains more to be settled, before we proceed to the meaning of the whole, and that is, the explanation of the second representation of a "good-for-nothing"* shepherd. The preceding statements, that the regular shepherds of Israel should be cut off, as it is said, "Three shepherds also I cut off in one month," i. e., in a very short time—and that the good shepherd should give up his office before the good-for-nothing shepherd arises, point us unequivocally, to those lawless and wicked leaders of the Jewish factions, who usurped the power in the very last period of the national existence. This is also acknowledged by Abendana, in his notes to the Michlal Jophi; for, after interpreting the words, "Woe to the good-for-nothing shepherd" of King Agrippa, he adds, "They are also spoken in reference to John, and Simon, and Eleazar, the princes of the robbers, who caused and wrought all the great evils that were done in Jerusalem."†

Having settled these preliminaries, we now return to consider the meaning of the whole chapter. It consists of two parts; the first, from verse 1—4, containing a verbal prophecy of the coming destruction; the second, from verse 5—17, a symbolic prophecy of the particulars. The first part is plain, and, therefore needs no comment. The second part subdivides into—first, the symbol of the good shepherd; and, secondly, of the foolish shepherd; of which we give the following paraphrase. Thus saith the Lord God to the Messiah, Feed my people Israel, the flock of slaughter; for I will no more pity them. And so Messiah undertook the office of shepherd. Instead of one shepherd's staff, he took two; the one to protect them

* Our translators have "idol shepherd;" but אֱלִיל signifies, first, "good for nothing," "of no value," as Kimchi has shown in the Commentary, by a reference to Job.

† ועוד אמר זה על יוחנן ושמעון ואלעזר שרי הפריצים אשר סבבו ועשו את כל הרעות הגדולות הנעשות בירושלים :

from foreign foes; the other, from intestine feuds. But the other shepherds, who had previously had the care of the flock, hated him: "My soul loathed them, and their soul also abhorred me;" so he gave them all three over to speedy destruction;* and at last was compelled to give up his office, for none but the poor acknowledged him. "The poor of the flock that waited upon me, knew that it was the word of the Lord." To show them their ingratitude to the Messiah, the symbolical shepherd asks them for payment, "Give me my price." But they, in derision, offer him the value of a common slave, "thirty pieces of silver," which the Lord commands him to cast to the potter, i. e., to an unclean place, just as Jeremiah had been commanded to break the potter's vessel in the valley of the son of Hinnom" (Jer. xix.). Zechariah, to make the matter visible to the people, casts it down in the house of the Lord for the potter, and breaks his two staves, to show that Messiah's care of the people should cease, and that then they should be given up to foreign enemies and civil dissensions. He then having finished the symbolical representation of the good shepherd the Messiah, proceeds to take the implements of a foolish shepherd, to show that, as they rejected the care of the Mes-

* We have seen above in the Commentary, that R. Abraham of Toledo explains the words, "Three shepherds also I cut off in one month," of the destruction of the three dynasties, the principality of David, the monarchy of the Hasmoneans, and the kingdom of Herod's family, during the existence of the second temple, of which he says, "He calls the whole duration of the second temple "one month," because it was in his sight "a few days." But it is plain from what is said above, that this must also refer to the destruction of the rulers and governors immediately before the destruction. Lightfoot thinks that the three shepherds mean, the Pharisees, the Sadducees, and the Essenes. But I rather think with Hengstenberg, that it refers to the prophets, priests, and civil rulers, who were essentially the shepherds of Israel. All three are enumerated to signify the total destruction of the Jewish polity.

siah, they should feel the yoke of wicked and ungodly men. This prediction, then, informs us, first, That before the destruction of Jerusalem, the Messiah should appear as shepherd of the people. Secondly, That none but the poor should attend to his words. Thirdly, That the rulers of the people, the shepherds, should "abhor" him, and should, therefore, be deprived of their power. Fourthly, That the Messiah should be valued at the price of a common slave. Fifthly, and lastly, That the people should, for their sin, be torn by civil feuds, and oppressed by ungodly rulers. The great question then, is, whether these particulars have been fulfilled in the history of Jesus of Nazareth. The most superficial knowledge of the Gospel will compel us to answer in the affirmative. Jesus of Nazareth did appear before the destruction of the second temple. He was rejected by the great and learned, but "the common people heard him gladly." He was hated and persecuted by the rulers, but in a short time their power was annihilated by the total destruction of the Jewish commonwealth. He was valued exactly at the sum of thirty pieces of silver, and the money, after being cast down in the temple, as a public reproof to the people, was devoted to a ceremonially unclean purpose, the purchase of the potter's field as a burial-place. And, lastly, confusion, anarchy, and slaughter, were the awful consequences of his rejection. The prophecy is sufficiently obscure, except when illustrated by the fulfilment, to prevent the possibility of a fraudulent adaptation of the history. The excessive difficulty which the rabbies found in interpreting it, and the wide difference of their sentiments as to the meaning, show that it is not a passage that would readily occur to an impostor: and the nature of the circumstances predicted, rendered the acomplishment impossible by the will of any such character. The valuation at thirty pieces of silver, depended on the will of the rulers; the rejection by all but the poor of the flock was not in his own power. The purchase of the potter's field was the act of the council. Put all these minute details together, and the conclusion must be, that the history of Jesus is authentic, and that it accurately fulfils the prophecy. But if not, then the prophecy has never been fulfilled, and the words of the prophet are found false.

If, therefore, there had been no allusion to this prophecy in the New Testament, the mere Gospel narrative would have led us to see that it was fulfilled in the history of Jesus. But Matthew expressly cites it; for after narrating that the thirty pieces of silver were applied to the purchase of the potter's field, and that this field was called "the field of blood," he adds, "Then was fulfilled that which was spoken by Jeremy, the prophet, saying, And they took the thirty pieces of silver, the price of him that was valued, whom they of the children of Israel did value, and gave them for the potter's field, as the Lord appointed me" (Matt. xxvii. 9, 10). This citation is, however, made the ground of an objection against St. Matthew. It is said, first, that he quotes the words of the Old Testament inaccurately; and, secondly, that he falsely ascribes the words of Zechariah to Jeremiah. We reply, in the first place, that even admitting, for the sake of argument, that both charges are true, they will not in any wise invalidate the claims of Jesus of Nazareth. Whether St. Matthew was or was not mistaken, we have already shown that his history exactly agrees with the Hebrew prediction. Whatever then, may become of St. Matthew, Jesus is the person of whom Zechariah spake, that is, he is the Messiah. If we should admit that St. Matthew was so ignorant as to quote Jeremiah instead of Zechariah, it is plain that we must acquit him of all fraudulent alteration of the text; for if he did not know the author of the words which he was quoting, it is certain that he could not have gone to the original in order to falsify it. And if he was, generally, so ignorant of prophecy, it is equally plain, that he could not have falsified the history, in order to make it agree with prophecy, of which he was ignorant: he is, therefore, a most unexceptionable witness as to the facts which he relates; and the ignorance of St. Matthew, if admitted, would thus render the proof from prophecy doubly cogent. Either the Jews must admit that he was acquainted with the prophecies, and then they must acquit him of mistake; or they must acknowledge that he was ignorant of the prophecies, and thus add to the weight of his testimony as to the facts which fulfilled the prediction. But, in the second place, we deny both charges. We say of the first, that he did not quote inaccurately, but that he intentionally gave the sense of the passage, instead of citing it verbatim; and that this mode of citation is fully justified, not only by the rabbies, but by the inspired writers of the Old Testament. Nehemiah says, "Remember, I beseech thee, the word that thou commandedst thy servant Moses, saying, If ye transgress, I will scatter you abroad among the nations; but if ye turn unto me, and keep my commandments, and do them; though there were of you cast out unto the uttermost part of the heaven, yet will I gather them from thence, and will bring them unto the place that I have chosen to set my name there" (Neh. i. 8, 9.). Now there is no such passage in the law, though there are several, of which it gives the sense. Compare also chapter x. 34—38, where the same method of citation appears. Daniel also, in his prayer, proves that the predictions of Moses were accomplished in the calamities that had come upon the Jews, and yet does not accurately cite the words of any one, but contents himself with giving the sense. "Therefore the curse is poured upon us, and the oath that is written in the law of Moses, the servant of God, because we have sinned against him.

And he hath confirmed his words which he spake against us, and against our judges that judged us, by bringing upon us a great evil; for under the whole heaven hath not been done as hath been done upon Jerusalem; as it is written in the law of Moses, All this evil hath come upon us," &c. What, therefore, is esteemed perfectly consistent with the character for inspiration of the Old Testament writers, can never be charged as a fault upon St. Matthew.

As to the second charge, several answers have been given, any one of which is sufficient to vindicate the character of St. Matthew. It has been said, that the abbreviations for Jeremiah and Zechariah, Ζϱιου and Iϱιου, are so alike as to be easily mistaken by the copier of the MS. It has been urged that some copies do really read "Zechariah," or, that in the original there was no prophet named, and that this mistake arose from the insertion of a marginal gloss. But Hengstenberg, following a hint thrown out by Grotius, appears to me to give the true answer; and that is, that St. Matthew intentionally ascribed the words of Zechariah to Jeremiah, because he wished to impress upon his readers the fact, that Zechariah's prediction was a reiteration of two fearful prophecies of Jeremiah (Jer. xviii. xix.), and should, like them, be accomplished in the rejection and destruction of the Jewish people. He wished to remind them, that "The field of blood," purchased with the money that testified the fulness of their guilt, was a part of that valley of the son of Hinnom, which their fathers had made a "field of blood" before them, and where Jeremiah had twice, by the symbol of a potter's vessel, announced their coming destruction. The words of the prophet, "Cast it to the potter," were in themselves sufficient to direct the attention of readers acquainted with the prophecies, to those two chapters of Jeremiah; but the manner in which St. Matthew introduces his quotation, makes the allusion still more plain. He first relates the purchase of the potter's field, thereby pointing out the locality of Jeremiah's prophecy—then he mentions the fact that it was called " the field of blood," thereby referring to a very similar expression in that prophet; " Behold the days come, saith the Lord, that this place shall no more be called Tophet, nor the valley of the son of Hinnom, but The valley of slaughter" (Jer. xix. 6.); and then cites the words of Zechariah, as spoken by Jeremiah, in order to make all mistake impossible. St. Matthew had, therefore, a direct purpose in introducing the name of Jeremiah; it was to warn the Jews against the coming judgments. They fondly hoped that, as the chosen people of God, they were safe. St. Matthew points them to the potter's field, and thus reminds them of the calamities which had already come upon them for past sin, less heinous than that of which the potter's field now testified.

CHAPTER XII.

1. "*The burden of the word of the Lord.*"—After mentioning the punishments of Israel, and the several desolations of the land, he prophecies concerning the good of Israel, and the punishments of the nations, and says, "Thus saith the Lord, which stretcheth forth the heavens, and layeth the foundations of the earth;" i. e., He created the heavens and the earth, and the universe is in his hand, to pull down and to throw down, to build and to plant. "Man" is mentioned, as Isaiah says, "I have made the earth, and created man upon it" (xiv. 12): that is to say, And I led Israel captive, and it is in my hand to lead them up from captivity, and to take vengeance on their enemies. The wise man, R. Abraham ben Ezra, of blessed memory, has written, that the words "And formeth the spirit of man within him," are connected with "stretching forth the heavens, and laying the foundations of the earth," because man is a little world, as the heavens and the earth are the great world. As to these words, וְיוֹצֵר רוּחַ אָדָם בְּקִרְבּוֹ, we do not find the word יצר, except of things which have solidity and are perceptible to the senses, which the Spirit, רוּחַ, is not. These words therefore, are spoken in reference to the formation of the organs of the body which receive the power of the Spirit, and these are the marrow and the heart.

2. "*Behold I ——— a cup of trembling.*"—סַף רַעַל is similar to כּוֹס הַתַּרְעֵלָה, "a cup of trembling," which he that drinks dies; so all that go up against Jerusalem shall perish and be cut off.

"*And also against Judah shall it be in the siege;*" that is to say, that Judah will be joined with the enemies in the siege against Jerusalem. And the meaning of the words "against Judah" is, that the cup of trembling shall be at first upon them, when they come against their will to besiege Jerusalem, and behold this great affliction shall be upon them. The sense of the whole passage is, That when Gog and Magog come against Jerusalem after the redemption, they will go up by the land of Judah, for the desire of their faces will be to come against Jerusalem first, and they will not be anxious first to subdue the whole land of Israel, for they will think, when we have subdued Jerusalem, the whole land will fall before us. But they will go up to Jerusalem by the way of the land of Judah, which is their natural route, and they will take with them the children of Judah against their will to go with them to besiege Jerusalem; and so Jonathan has interpreted.

3. "*And it shall come to pass, in that day I will make Jerusalem a burdensome stone.*"

He first compared it to "a cup of trembling;" he now further compares it to a burdensome stone, i. e. all who labour to make war against Jerusalem shall be punished by it, as a great stone which is to them that burden themselves with it a great burden and a heavy weight; and even in raising it from the ground to place it on their shoulders, they cut their hands with it, and many men exhaust their strength, and in moving it cut their hands; thus all the Gentiles of the earth shall be gathered against Jerusalem, and shall be destroyed by the Lord.

מַעֲמָסָה, "burden," is from עמס, as וַיַּעֲמֹס אִישׁ עַל־חֲמֹרוֹ "And every man loaded his ass" (Gen. xliv. 13.). And again, וְעֹמְסִים עַל־הַחֲמֹרִים, "and lading asses" (Nehem. xiii. 15). The word expresses the idea of burden. Jonathan has interpreted it, "I will make Jerusalem a stumbling-stone to all nations. All who do violence to it shall assuredly be spoiled."

4. "*In that day* —— *I will open my eyes,*" to keep

them from the smiting which I will bring upon the nations. Although they be amongst them, they and their horses, they shall be delivered from the smiting, but I will smite every horse of the nations with blindness. "Blindness" is mentioned after "madness," for they shall be smitten with these two plagues. Madness applies to the heart, and blindness to the eyes.

5. "*And the governors of Judah shall say in their heart;*" i.e. when in the midst of their enemies, they shall say that the inhabitants of Jerusalem are a strength and defence to them, for they shall go forth to fight with them in the help of the Lord of hosts, and by them they shall be delivered.

אַמְצָה, "strength," is a noun of the same form as עַוְלָה (unrighteousness), עַנְוָה (humility), כַּבְשָׂה (a lamb), שַׁלְוָה (prosperity).

6. "*In that day the governors of Judah.*"—The great men of Judah who are outside I will make like a hearth of fire among the wood, for by the fire which I shall send among the Gentiles is meant the madness and blindness, for it is from the Lord. And they and the children of Judah who are with them shall smite the Gentiles on the right hand and on the left. The meaning of כִּיוֹר אֵשׁ is "a coal of fire." It belongs to such words as תַּנּוּר and כִּירַיִם, furnace and oven, for as the wood and the sheaf are ready to be kindled by the fire, so the heathen shall be ready for destruction and consumption by the madness and insanity which the blessed God shall send amongst them; and the governors of Judah shall be in the midst of them like fire to consume them.

"*And Jerusalem shall be inhabited again in her own place, even in Jerusalem.*"—For the Gentiles thought to annihilate it from being a city, but it shall be inhabited again in its own place, the place that in this day is called Jerusalem.

7. "*The Lord also will save the tents of Judah first.*"

—As the besiegers of the city dwell in tents, therefore he mentions "the tents of Judah." Some say that this refers to the house of the Rechabites, for they dwell in tents for ever, and they were living amongst the children of Judah. Jonathan has interpreted "the tents of Judah" by "the cities of the house of Judah."

"*First.*"—Before the inhabitants of Jerusalem are saved, the children of Judah, who are outside, shall be saved from the fear of their enemies with whom they came to the siege.

"*That the glory of the house of David* —— *do not magnify themselves.*"—For the house of David will be inside the city with the inhabitants of Jerusalem, and if they should be saved first, they would boast themselves over the children of Judah, who are outside, and would say that by their hand they have been saved.

8. "*In that day* —— *the stumbler amongst them.*"—He that is weak amongst them, shall be as David, who was a mighty man of valour and a man of war.

"*And the house of David,*" i. e. the King the Messiah, as "Hear ye now, O house of David" (Isa. vii. 13) is said of Ahaz the king. And the king shall go out before them to fight against those nations.

"*As God.*"—The explanation follows, "As the angel of the Lord."

9. "*And it shall come to pass in that day, I will seek to destroy.*"—I will seek and I will do; that is to say, I will make it all my pleasure to destroy them.

10. "*And I will pour* —— *the spirit of grace and supplications.*"—i. e. They shall find grace in my sight, and I will save them from the Gentiles who come against them. He repeats the same thing in different words, for the sake of confirmation. Jonathan has interpreted it, "The spirit of grace and mercy." My lord my father, of blessed memory, has interpreted this, "that they shall have favour in the eyes of every man, and that their

prayers shall be accepted before me." And behold he says that he will defend them. Behold he had mentioned the highest degrees that exalt them; afterwards he says if it should happen that they pierce any one of them in the war, even a common man, there will be a great astonishment amongst them how this thing could happen; and they will look upon it as the beginning of a fall and defeat before their enemies; as Joshua did when the men of Ai smote thirty-six men of Israel. He said, "Alas! O Lord God, what shall I say when Israel turn their backs before their enemies" (Josh. vii. 8). The feeling will be similar at that time, if they should see any one of theirs pierced: though it should be only one, they will wonder.

"*And they shall look upon me whom they have pierced,*" because they have pierced.

"*And they shall mourn for him,*" as a man that has only one son and he dies, or as a man whose firstborn dies. Our rabbies, of blessed memory, have interpreted this of Messiah, the son of Joseph, who shall be killed in the war. But I wonder, according to their interpretation, how he is here spoken of unconnectedly, without any previous mention at all.

הָמֵר signifies bitterness, grief of heart.

11. "*In that day ——— as the mourning.*"—כְּמִסְפַּד is pointed with Pathach on account of the Regimen.

"*Hadadrimmon in the valley of Megiddon.*"—It was known to them, but we have not seen any mention of it in the Bible.

12. "*And the land shall mourn.*"—The men of the land shall mourn on account of this piercing.

"*Every family apart.*"—Each in its place. The families here mentioned, as Nathan and Shimei, will be great and known at that time, and the prophet mentions them prophetically. And that which is said, "and their wives apart," is for the sake of modesty. Or the meaning may be, that as the women lament and mourn more than the men, it is said, that the women shall be gathered together apart to mourn according to their manner.

OBSERVATIONS ON CHAPTER XII. 10.

Kimchi, as we have seen in the Commentary, differs from our translators as to the sense of the words וְהִבִּיטוּ אֵלַי אֵת אֲשֶׁר דָּקָרוּ, which they have rendered, "And they shall look upon me whom they have pierced," but which he would translate, "They shall look upon (or unto) me, because they have pierced, בעבור שדקרו." Now, whatever be the sense of the words, it is plain that Kimchi is in error; for according to his sense, the transitive verb דָּקָרוּ, "they pierced," is left without an accusative case, and the whole sentence is deprived of meaning. Just read the whole verse according to this translation: "I will pour upon the house of David, and upon the inhabitants of Jerusalem, the spirit of grace and of supplications; and they shall look upon me because they pierced, and they shall mourn for him as one mourneth for his only son," &c. The mere inspection of the words is sufficient to show that this translation is wrong; and it cannot be pretended that the accusative case is omitted, for in every other passage where the verb דָּקַר occurs, the accusative is plainly expressed. The fact is, however, that Kimchi intended to insinuate more than he has expressed. He meant to make the words אֵת אֲשֶׁר ("whom") signify not simply "because," but "because of him whom," so that the whole sense should be, "They shall look to me because of him whom they pierced:" and thus R. Isaac, who follows Kimchi, fairly gives it. He says, "*Whom they pierced*, means, *Because of him whom they pierced.* אֵת אֲשֶׁר in this place has the meaning of *because*, בעבור, as in those words of Ezekiel (xxxvi. 27), אֵת אֲשֶׁר בְּחֻקַּי תֵּלֵכוּ, [which he appears to translate, 'Because ye walk in my statutes']." * But this honesty of R. Isaac at once furnishes the reply, and shows why Kimchi contented himself with an insinuation. By saying that אֵת אֲשֶׁר [whom] signifies "because of," the latter preserved an appearance of truth. But by asserting that it signifies, "Because of him whom," the latter betrays the untenableness of the proposed interpretation. The truth is, that אֵת אֲשֶׁר may sometimes signify, "because," but never does mean, "Because of him whom." For instance, in Levit. xxvi. 35, "As long as it lieth desolate it shall rest; אֵת אֲשֶׁר, *because* it did not rest in your Sabbaths, when ye dwelt upon it." Here we have the sense "because;" but it cannot thence be inferred that it also signifies "because of him whom." This translation, therefore, as leaving דָּקָרוּ without an accusative case, shows that it is incorrect, whilst the fact that this verb must have an object, and that if אֵת אֲשֶׁר be not the accusative, it has none, proves that our translation, "whom," is necessarily correct. But even should we admit the translation, still Kimchi's interpretation of the whole verse would be far from the truth. It is thus given in the Chizzuk Emunah, "If it should happen that any of the Israelites should be pierced, namely, in that war, even though it should be one of the most inconsiderable, they shall wonder greatly how this could happen, and will think that this is the beginning of a fall and defeat before their enemies, as Joshua did, When the men of Ai smote thirty-six of Israel, he said, 'Alas, O Lord God, why didst thou cause this people to pass the Jordan.' And again, 'What shall I say, when Israel turn their backs before their enemies' (Josh. vii.). So will it be at that time, if they should see any of them pierced, they will be

* Tela Ignea, part ii. p. 308.

astonished and look to me on account of him whom they have pierced." Now, in the first place, this interpretation introduces a new subject to the verb "pierce," for which there is no authority. No one who reads the words, "They shall look upon me on account of him whom they have pierced," would ever suppose that those who pierced are different from those who shall look; and still less that the one are the Gentiles, and the other the Jews. There is not the slightest intimation of a change of subject. The only persons spoken of are "The house of David and the inhabitants of Jerusalem." And, secondly, to suppose that when the Jews are in Jerusalem, and as Kimchi supposes, have the Messiah in the midst of them, and therefore must know that it is the time of their deliverance,—to suppose under such circumstances, that they should indulge in such excessive fear and grief because of the death of any obscure person, is perfectly absurd: and still more so to suppose that the outpouring of the Spirit of God should produce such manifest unbelief in God's promises. Kimchi and Rashi, of whose interpretation this is only a modification, must have felt a very urgent necessity for getting rid of the old opinion, that the person pierced was the Messiah, when they made up their minds to adopt so vapid an exposition. It has, however, failed in obtaining general adoption amongst the Jews. Some of the greatest names have declared against it. Aben Ezra, who wrote after Rashi had first started the idea; Abarbanel and Alshech, with Kimchi before them, have all rejected it, and assert, in conformity with the Talmud, that it refers to Messiah, the son of Joseph. Aben Ezra says, "All the heathen shall look to me to see what I shall do to those who pierced Messiah, the son of Joseph."* Abarbanel, after noticing the interpretations of Rashi and Kimchi, says, "It is more correct to interpret this passage of

* או יביטו כל הגוים אלי לראות מה אעשה לאלה אשר דקרו משיח בן יוסף׃

Messiah, the son of Joseph, as our rabbies of blessed memory have interpreted in the treatise Succah,* for he shall be a mighty man of valour, of the tribe of Joseph, and shall, at first, be captain of the Lord's host in that war, but in that war shall die." This second exposition, however, though nearer the truth than the former, is also untenable. Even if we were to admit a Messiah ben Joseph, this verse cannot possibly apply to him. Why should the house of David and the inhabitants of Jerusalem mourn so bitterly for a son of Joseph, especially as, according to Abarbanel, his death is to make way for the object of their hopes and prayers, Messiah, the son of David? "It is not meet," he says, "that any one should think, that the death of Messiah ben Joseph should be by chance. On the contrary, by the providence of God, and in order that the kingdom may return to the seed of David, Messiah ben Joseph shall die in that war in such a manner, as that Israel will say, Has he not been killed because, being of the tribe of Ephraim, he took to himself the crown of the kingdom?"† If this be true, instead of mourning, they would rejoice that the last obstacle to their long-expected felicity had been removed. Even on the showing of the rabbies themselves, the death of the Messiah ben Joseph must be an occasion of joy, not of grief, and therefore cannot be the event alluded to in this verse, which is of so distressing a nature, as to call forth the most vehement sorrow from those who had received the spirit of grace and supplications. But, secondly, there is no Messiah ben Joseph. To enter into the whole question of the two Messiahs here, would exceed the limits of these observations.

* Fol. 52, col. 1. ויותר נכון לפרשו על משיח בן יוסף כמו שפירשו רז'ל במס' סוכה לפי שהוא יהיה איש גבור חיל משבט יוסף ויהי' שר צבא ה' באותה מלחמה בראשונה והוא ימות באותה מלחמה ·

† ומיתת משיח בן יוסף אין ראוי שיחשוב אדם שתהיה מקרית אלא בהשגחת השם שכדי שתחזור המלוכה לזרע דוד ימות משיח בן יוסף במלחמה באופן שיאמרו ישראל הלא על כי לקח לו כתר המלוכה בהיותו משבט אפרים נהרג וכו' ·

Here let it suffice to say, that if there are two Messiahs, they must either be contemporary, or one must come after the other. But they cannot exist together, for Ezekiel promises, that when God saves his people, they shall have only one Shepherd, and that he shall be Messiah, the son of David. "Therefore will I save my flock, and they shall no more be a prey: and I will judge between cattle and cattle. And I will set up one shepherd, רֹעֶה אֶחָד, over them, and he shall feed them, even my servant David" (Ezek. xxxiv. 22, 23; compare also xxxvii. 21—24). Neither can they be in succession, for Hosea says expressly, that until they seek Messiah, the son of David, they shall have neither king nor prince. "For the children of Israel shall abide many days without a king and without a prince, אֵין מֶלֶךְ וְאֵין שָׂר ——— Afterwards shall the children of Israel return, and seek the Lord their God, and David their king: and shall fear the Lord and his goodness in the last days" (Hosea iii. 4, 5). In neither case, therefore, can there be two Messiahs: and therefore this passage of Zechariah cannot refer to Messiah, the son of Joseph.

It now remains only to consider the Christian interpretation, which is, that Messiah, the son of David, is the person pierced, and that the Israelites shall mourn because of the national and personal guilt incurred by piercing and rejecting him. That this is the true and obvious interpretation, appears,

First, from the Jewish tradition that the place refers to Messiah, the son of Joseph. It cannot be said that the disciples of Jesus of Nazareth found a passage that seemed to suit their purpose, and wrested it from the received exposition of the nation. On the contrary, their learned men were of opinion that this passage referred to a Messiah: and even after the New Testament had applied it to Jesus of Nazareth, and there was, therefore, a motive for rejecting their opinion, this exposition has still main tained its ground. Abarbanel, whose commentaries are avowedly controversial against Christianity, is still compelled by the context to apply the whole passage to the times of the Messiah, and to acknowledge that the person pierced is a Messiah. This fact shows, either that this exposition had taken such hold of the Jewish mind, as to make it impossible to get rid of it—or, that the sense of the passage is so obvious as to overcome even prejudice and inclination.

And, Secondly, this argument is much strengthened by the determination which Rashi displays to get rid of this explanation. In his commentary on the Bible, he denies that it applies to Messiah, the son of Joseph: but in his commentary on the Talmud, he asserts the correctness of the application. In the former he says, "They shall look back to mourn, because the Gentiles had pierced some amongst them, and killed some of them."* But in the latter he says, "The words, 'The land shall mourn,' are found in the prophecy of Zechariah, and he prophesies of the future, that they shall mourn on account of Messiah, the son of Joseph, who shall be slain in the war of Gog and Magog"† (Succah. fol. 52, col. 1). That this manifest contradiction is not accidental, but intentional, appears from the fact, that this writer has dealt similarly by other controverted passages; for instance, Isaiah liii., which, in his commentary on the Bible, he expounds of the Jewish people, but which, in his commentary on the Talmud,‡ he explains of Messiah. Indeed his determination to get rid of any explanation that could favour Christianity, is plainly avowed in his commentary on the xxist Psalm, where he says, "Our rabbies have expounded it of the King Messiah, but it is better to expound it

* והביטו להתאונן על אשר דקרו בהם האומו׳ והרגו מהם בגלותם:

† וספדה הארץ בנבואת זכריה ומתנבא לעתיד שיספדו על משיח בן יוסף שנהרג במלחמת גוג ומגוג׳

‡ Sanhedrin, fol. 93, col. 1.

further of David himself, in order to answer heretics" (see also Ps. ii., which he treats in the same way). Now, when an adversary is driven to deny in controversy what he elsewhere acknowledges to be true, he tacitly acknowledges the power of the argument which he thus tries to evade. Rashi's want of ingenuousness in the present instance is no small confirmation of the correctness and obviousness of the Christian exposition.

Thirdly, the Christian interpretation agrees with the context. The Jewish commentators all acknowledge, that the whole chapter refers to the times of the Messiah.

Fourthly, it connects naturally with the preceding and following words: "I will pour out upon the house of David, and the inhabitants of Jerusalem, the spirit of grace and supplication: and they shall look upon me whom they have pierced, and they shall mourn for him as one mourneth for his only son," &c. The looking and the mourning are represented as the consequences of the outpouring of the Spirit, but elsewhere true repentance is represented as the fruits of this spiritual influence, as in Ezek. xxxvi. 25—31, where, after the promise of the Spirit, the prophet adds, "Then shall ye remember your own evil ways, and your doings that were not good, and shall loathe yourselves in your own sight, for your iniquities and your abominations:" which would lead us to infer, that the great mourning over him that was pierced is the sorrow of repentance; and which is rendered still more probable by the further effect described in the xiiith chapter, namely, the cessation of idols and of false prophets. Now, on the Christian hypothesis, this is perfectly intelligible and consistent. The Jews rejected and pierced the Messiah, and therefore, when the Spirit is poured out, they will repent and mourn in bitterness of soul over him whom they pierced. Here is a cause adequate to the profundity of the grief, and a result exactly corresponding with the gift of the Spirit.

Every word in the passage has its full force, and the connexion is easy and natural. Indeed so natural is this sense, that it has been seen by one of the most celebrated rabbies. Alshech, in his Commentary on Zechariah, has the following remarkable passage:—"I will do yet a third thing, and that is, that 'they shall look unto me,' for they shall lift up their eyes unto me in perfect repentance, when they see him whom they pierced, that is Messiah, the son of Joseph; for our rabbies, of blessed memory, have said, that he will take upon himself all the guilt of Israel, and shall then be slain in the war to make an atonement, in such a manner, that it shall be accounted as if Israel had pierced him, for on account of their sin he has died; and therefore, in order that it may be reckoned to them as a perfect atonement, they will repent, and look to the blessed One, saying that there is none beside Him to forgive those that mourn on account of him who died for their sin: this is the meaning of 'They shall look upon me.'"* Excepting the mention of Messiah ben Joseph, the rabbi has exactly given the Christian sense.

There is but one objection that can be made to the Christian interpretation, and that is, that the Christian version makes God himself the victim whom they pierced, but that shall be considered in the observations on the next chapter.

* ועוד שלישי' אעשה והיא כי הביטו אלי שיתלו עיניהם אלי בתשובה שלימה וראותם אשר דקרו הוא משיח בן יוסף שאז"ל שיקבל על עצמו כל אשמו' יש' ויהרג אז במלחמ' לכפר בעד באופן שיחשב כאלו יש' דקרו אותו כי בחטאתם מת ועל כן למען יחשב להם לכפרה שלימה יעשו תשובה והביטו אליו ית' באמור כי אין זולתו למחול למתאבלים על אשר מת בעונם וזהו והביטו אלי את וכו'

CHAPTER XIII.

1. "*In that day there shall be a fountain opened to the house of David.*"—It is possible that this is to be interpreted according to its literal sense, and so our rabbies, of blessed memory, have connected it with the verse, "Living waters shall go forth from Jerusalem." (ch. xiv.) They have said it may be interpreted that other springs shall be mixed with them. But the words, "there shall be a fountain opened to the house of David," show that it is only one fountain for sin and for uncleanness. They have further said, that when the waters reach the door of the house of David, they become a great river, for it is said, "In that day there shall be a fountain opened to the house of David." And so far as the verse is interpreted literally, then the meaning of the words, "for sin and for uncleanness" will be, that before that day no waters went forth in Jerusalem in the midst of the city, but then living waters shall go forth in the city, and they shall not be obliged to go forth outside the city for the waters of purification, for which living water is required, as it is written; and thus also for her that labours under uncleanness for whom living water is necessary.

2. "*And it shall come to pass ——— I will cut off the names of the idols,*" either of those that were there formerly before their captivity, or the idols which the uncircumcised worship there at this day.

"*And the prophets also.*"—The false prophets who were there during the first temple.

"*And the unclean spirit.*"—The evil affection יצר הרע.

"3. "*And it shall come to pass, when any shall yet prophesy.*"—I will cause the prophets to pass out, but if there should be a sinner who will prophesy by a lying spirit, and lie, and say that he prophesies by the Spirit of God, Israel shall at that time possess such knowledge and understanding, that they will recognise the words of that prophet whether they be lies or truth: and his father and mother that begat him shall say to him, Thou shalt not live, for thou speakest lies in the name of the Lord.

"*That begat him.*"—This is to make the matter clearer, for he had already mentioned his father and mother.

"*His father and his mother shall thrust him through.*"—They shall beat him and wound him to chastise him, or the meaning of "shall thrust him through" is, They shall kill him; as it is said, Thou shalt not live.

4. "*And it shall come to pass in that day, they shall be ashamed.*"—When they see that their prophecies are not fulfilled, they shall be ashamed.

בְּהִנָּבְאֹתוֹ is the infinitive with the addition of ת. And so in the Mishna is a similar form להבראות in the words,

הוא במאמר אחד יכול להבראות.*

"*Neither shall they wear a garment of hair to deceive.*"—This was the custom of the false prophets to wear sackcloth, or a garment of hair.

"*In order to deceive.*—That they may be able to deceive, and that the children of men may believe in them: for they show themselves before the children of men that they are separate,† and righteous, and upright men, and that would not speak lies. But when they see that their prophecy is not fulfilled, they shall have shame, and leave off their deeds, and their visions, and their garments, and shall deny their prophecy, and shall say that they are not prophets, and have never prophesied, but are tillers of the ground. They shall not busy themselves with these things, but with the tilling of the ground, and with cattle and property.

* Pirke Avoth. c. v. 1.

† Literally Pharisees.

5. "*But he shall say.*"—He shall say to him that asks him, where is his prophecy. He shall deny and say, I am not a Prophet.

הִקְנַנִי.—He taught me to be a shepherd of cattle, and to employ myself with tilling the ground.

6. "*And one shall say to him, What are these wounds in thy hands?*"—If it be so, that thou hast not been a prophet, what are these wounds in thy hands, for the wounds are a sign that thou hast prophesied, and that thy father and mother have smitten thee and chastised thee, that thou shouldest not prophesy.

"*Those with which I was wounded in the house of my friends.*"—He shall say, these wounds are not on account of prophecy, but my friends wounded and chastised me because I was abandoned, and was not industrious in cultivating the land in my youth, and they beat me that I should cease from the profligacy of young men, and should set to my work. And the reason of the wounds being in the hands is, that they used to bind his hands and feet that he should not go out.

The sense of the whole passage refers to the future, for God has appointed as to the future, and has said, "It shall come to pass afterwards, that I will pour out my Spirit upon all flesh, and your sons and your daughters shall prophesy," &c. (Joel). But those persons who cannot prophesy will envy the others who can prophesy, and will make themselves prophets like the others, but their fathers who hear their prophecy will know that it is a lie, and will say to them, Thou shalt not live, for thou hast spoken lies in the name of the Lord. But my lord, my father, may his memory be blessed, has interpreted this of the future, in the time of the resurrection, and has said, "When the dead live, as is written in Daniel, Many of them that sleep in the dust of the earth shall awake, some to everlasting life, i. e., the righteous, and some to everlasting shame and contempt, i. e., Those who have denied a fundamental article, and who deny the resurrection of the dead, and those middle sort of persons who have not denied a fundamental article, but have been dreamers of false dreams, and have prophesied out of their own heart, but have not committed idolatry; when these persons live again, there will be marks in their hands, like the marks of an ulcer, or the itch. And this will be the reward of their deeds and the punishment of their lying prophecy, that the children of men shall recognise it, and they shall have shame, as it is said, "The prophets shall be ashamed every one of his vision when he prophesied," on account of his false prophecy in former days. "And they shall no longer wear a garment of hair, as they did at first when they used to wear sackcloth and the clothes of the separate, and of the servants of God, that the children of men might believe their lies. But in the time to come when the children of men shall see and know them, each one of them will deny and say, the things have never been, for I was an husbandman."

"*For man taught me to keep cattle from my youth.*"—אָדָם means an amhaaretz, unlearned man. הִקְנַנִי made me a shepherd of cattle and an husbandman; and when they say to him, What are these wounds in thine hands? he will say, they are those with which I was wounded in the house of my friends, in the Beth Hamedrash (house of study) my friends beat me on account of my writing, when we used to write, or were learning, or some such thing.

7. "*Awake, O sword, against my shepherd.*"—Rashi, of blessed memory, has interpreted this, "Against the prince whom I have appointed over my sheep of the captivity;" and, "Against the man that is my fellow," whom I have associated to myself to keep my flock as I do.

"*Smite the shepherd.*"—The wicked prince. But the wise man, R. Abraham Aben Ezra, has interpreted this prophecy of the great wars which shall be in all the world in the days of the Messiah, the son of Joseph. And the meaning of "my shepherd" is, Every king of the Gentiles whom God has caused to rule over the earth, and he thinks himself to be as God, therefore he says, "Against the man my fellow;" i. e., who thinks of himself that he is my fellow.

"*Smite the Shepherd.*"—God, blessed be He, will cut off every king from the Gentiles, and his flock shall be scattered. "The little ones" are the governors and princes, who are less than the kings. Jonathan has interpreted, "O sword, be revealed against the king," &c.; i. e., those who are next to the kings and the governors.

8. "*And it shall come to pass in all the land.*"—In all the land of Israel. And some interpret, in the whole world, for even of the nations none will be left, but those who are good and serve God.

פִּי שְׁנַיִם.—Two parts of them.

"*Shall be cut off shall die.*"—Some of them shall be cut off by the sword, and some shall die by the pestilence.

"*But the third shall be left therein.*"—Shall remain in the land of the living.

9. "*And I will bring them through the fire.*"—Through severe afflictions like unto fire. And fire is mentioned, because the figure is taken from a refiner of silver and gold, for they refine and prove it with fire. Thus they shall be refined and proved by bearing severe afflictions cheerfully at the time when they bear them. Jonathan also has thus translated, "I will bring the third part into affliction in a furnace of fire."

OBSERVATIONS ON CHAPTER XIII. 7—9.

In attempting to vindicate the Christian interpretation of this remarkable passage, "Awake, O sword, against my shepherd, and against the man that is my fellow, saith the Lord of hosts," we are spared the trouble of defending our translation. The rabbies understand the words, and construe the whole passage as we do. We can, therefore, proceed at once to the interpretation, respecting which the rabbies all differ one from the other. Kimchi, as we have seen in the Commentary, interprets "my shepherd," of "every king of the Gentiles, whom God has caused to rule over the earth, and who thinks himself as God. Therefore it is said, 'Against the man my fellow;' i. e., who thinks of himself that he is my fellow." R. Isaac, the author of the Chizzuk Emunah, says that these words mean, "Awake, O sword, against the King of Ishmael, called also the King of Turkey, and ruling over Asia and Africa, under whose hand the majority of the people of Israel are in captivity. God calls him 'my shepherd,' because He has given His sheep into his hand, to feed them in their captivity. 'The sheep' mean Israel. He calls him 'The man my fellow,' and companion, because, in the pride and haughtiness of his heart, he thinks himself like God, and similar to this is that passage, 'Behold, the man is become as one of us.' "* Abarbanel confesses that this passage puzzles him, for he offers three different interpretations. He says, "It appears to me that the words 'Awake, O sword, against my shepherd, and the man that is my fellow,' may be interpreted in one of three ways. The first, that as the prophets of the Gentiles and their saints and devout persons will say, that they inherited lies, and that they wish to be 'husbandmen,' or feeders of sheep, as Rashi

* Tela ignea, p. ii., page 310.

has explained on the words 'Man hath taught me to keep cattle' (verse 5), therefore God says, with reference to that prophet, who wishes to make himself a shepherd, 'Awake, O sword, against my shepherd,' that is to say, the sword shall come upon that shepherd who was in his own eyes formerly 'a man, my fellow,' near to me, and adhering to me, but now makes himself a shepherd, &c."* "The second mode of interpretation, and that which is more appropriate in my eyes, is that the words 'my shepherd' are spoken of the prophet of the Ishmaelites, whom they call Mahomet, of whom they say that God sent him into the world to feed his sheep, the children of men; and that the words 'the man my fellow,' are spoken of Jesus the Nazarene, for, according to the sentiments of the children of Edom, and their faith, he was the Son of God, and of the same substance, and therefore he is called according to their words, 'The man my fellow,' &c." † "The third interpretation is, that the words 'my shepherd, the man my fellow,' are spoken of Messiah, the son of Joseph, &c." ‡ These interpretations necessarily destroy one another. This diversity shows the great difficulty which the rabbies found in getting any interpretation that would satisfy their understanding, as is especially apparent in Abarbanel, a man of great learning and consummate talent; and yet so far is he from being satisfied either with what his predecessors had written, or he himself could devise, that he proposes

* נראה לי לפרשו באחד משלשה פנים האחד כי לפי שאמר שנביאי הגוים וקדושיו ופרושיו יאמרו ששקר נחלו ושהם רוצים להיות עובדי אדמה או רועי צאן כפי מה שפרש"י במל' הקנני מלשון מקנה לכן אמר השם כנגד אותו הנבי' שרוצה לעשות עצמו רועה חרב עורי על רועי ר"ל חרב תבוא על הרועה הזה שבראשונ' היה בעיניו גבר עמיתי קרוב אלי ודבק בי ועתה עושה עצמו רועה וכו'

† והאופן השני מהפירוש והוא היותר נכון בעיני הוא שאמר רועי על נביא הישמעאלים הנקרא אצלם מחמד שאומרי' ששלחו השם בעולם לרעו' את צאנו בני אדם ושאמר גבר עמיתי על ישו הנוצרי שכפי מחשבת בני אדום ואמונתם הוא היה בן האל עצם מעצמיו ולכן קראו גבר עמיתי כפי דבריהם וכו'

‡ והפן השלישי מהפירוש הוא שאמר רועי וגבר עמיתי על משיח בן יוסף וכו'

three interpretations, and does not venture to decide upon any one as certain and true. Such diversity and doubt is a strong presumption against them all, and an examination of the passage shows that they are decidedly false. The first step is to ascertain who are meant by "The sheep," in the words "Smite the shepherd, and the sheep shall be scattered." Do they represent Israel or the Gentiles? The whole Old Testament testifies that where shepherd and sheep are used figuratively, the sheep represent Israel. Thus Moses, when praying for a successor, gives us the reason, "That the congregation of the Lord be not as sheep which have no shepherd" (Numb. xxvii. 17). The Psalms are full of this figure, as, "We are the people of his pasture, and the sheep of his hand" (xcv. 7). And again, "We are his people, and the sheep of his pasture" (c. 3). And so are the prophets, as "He that scattered Israel will gather him, and keep him as a shepherd doth his flock" (Jer. xxxi. 10). And again, "As a shepherd seeketh out his flock in the day that he is among his sheep that are scattered: so will I seek out my sheep, and will deliver them out of all places whither they have been scattered in the dark and cloudy day" (Ezek. xxxiv. 7). Similar passages are so many and so plain, that we must come to the same conclusion as R. Isaac, in the citation given above, that "sheep" mean Israel: and therefore the scattering of the sheep means the scattering of Israel, and therefore the smiting of the shepherd, whoever he be, must have taken place before Israel was scattered: and therefore all the Rabbinic interpretations which refer the smiting of the shepherd to the time to come are false. In the time to come, Israel is not to be scattered, but to be gathered. The scattering took place nearly 1800 years ago, and antecedent to that event the shepherd must have been smitten; it therefore cannot mean the destruction of any Gentile kings, nor of Messiah ben Joseph in the time to come.

The next step is to inquire who is meant by "the shepherd." No particular epithet is added, and he may, therefore, either be a bad shepherd or a good shepherd. But, as the scattering of the flock is consequent upon his death, it follows, that before his death they were not scattered, but that, before he was smitten, he held them together. He cannot, therefore, be a bad shepherd; for the peculiar characteristic which the Scripture gives of a bad shepherd is, that he scatters the flock. Thus Jeremiah says, "Woe be unto the shepherds that destroy and scatter the sheep of my pasture! saith the Lord. Therefore thus saith the Lord God of Israel against the shepherds that feed my people, Ye have scattered my flock, and driven them away, and have not visited them: behold, I will visit upon you the evil of your doings, saith the Lord" (Jer. xxiii. 1, 2). As this shepherd then, kept them together, and did not suffer them to be scattered, until he was smitten, it follows that he must be a good shepherd. And therefore the words "My shepherd, the man that is my fellow," cannot be spoken ironically, but must be strictly applicable. "My shepherd" must designate some one peculiarly appointed by God to feed his flock; and, if we search the prophets, we shall find that He who is promised as the shepherd of Israel is the Messiah, as was shown at pages 142, 143. The Messiah, therefore, is the person to be smitten before the scattering of the sheep.

Such is the conclusion to which an examination of the passage itself, and a comparison of the language with that of the prophets, would lead, and this conclusion is rendered absolutely certain, by comparing Zechariah with himself. In the xith chapter we have seen the same figure employed. The people of Israel are compared to sheep committed to the care of a good shepherd, and when he ceases to perform the office, calamity and ruin are the consequence. The identity of the symbols and the things symbolized, in both visions, shows that they refer to the same persons and the same events. It is true that in the xith chapter, Zechariah does not mention the death of the Messiah, but he does in the xiith. "They shall look upon me whom they pierced"; and in both he intimates that the Messiah is a divine person, as God here calls him "The man that is my fellow." In xi. 13, we read "The LORD יהוה said unto me, Cast it unto the potter: a goodly price that I was prized at of them," where the Lord identifies himself with the shepherd. In xii. 10, He who pours out the Spirit of grace and supplication, identifies himself with Him that is pierced, so that the words under consideration, "The man that is my fellow," exactly agree with the character of Messiah, as previously given by Zechariah. That עמיתי, "my fellow," implies that He of whom it is spoken is a divine person, is plainly acknowledged by those rabbies who oppose Christianity. R. Isaac says, "He calls him 'The man, my fellow,' and companion, because in the pride and haughtiness of his heart, he thinks himself as it were God." And Abarbanel, who endeavours to interpret the words in a bad sense of our Lord, acknowledges still more plainly that these words signify one of the same substance. "The words, 'The man my fellow,' are spoken of Jesus the Nazarene, for, according to the sentiments of the children of Edom, and their faith, he was the Son of God, and of the same substance, and therefore he is called, according to their words, 'The man that is my fellow.'" He here plainly and positively asserts, that these words express the Christian doctrine of the Deity of Messiah, and thinks that they were selected on that account. These two testimonies of two controversialists, writing professedly against Christianity, are of the greatest value. They show that the grammatical sense assigned to the passage by Christians, and on which Christians rest their interpretation, is so obvious, and so necessarily true, that the most acute adversaries are compelled to admit it; and can only escape from it by saying that the words are ironical. This concession is rendered doubly valuable by the consideration that they had before them another explanation, proposed by a rabbi of great renown, and that they rejected it. Rashi, as quoted by Kimchi in the Commentary, page 167, says that kings are called God's fellows, because they are associated with him in feeding his sheep, but R. Isaac and Abarbanel preferred expounding עמיתי "My fellow," of a similarity in nature and substance; and, no doubt, their reason for this preference was the fact that, in all the other passages where it occurs, it can have no other meaning.* Except in this passage it only occurs in the Pentateuch as follows:—Levit. v. 20, (English, vi. 2), "If a soul sin, and commit a trespass against the Lord, and lie unto his neighbour or *fellow* בַּעֲמִיתוֹ in that which was delivered to him to keep, or in fellowship, or in a thing taken away by violence, or hath deceived his neighbour עֲמִיתוֹ."—Lev. xviii. 20, "Moreover, thou shalt not lie carnally with thy neighbour's wife אֵשֶׁת עֲמִיתְךָ."—xix. 11, "Ye shall not steal, neither deal falsely, neither lie one to another (a man with his neighbour) אִישׁ בַּעֲמִיתוֹ."—verse 15, "In righteousness shalt thou judge thy neighbour עֲמִיתְךָ."—verse 17, "Thou shalt not hate thy brother in thine heart; thou shalt not in any wise rebuke thy neighbour עֲמִיתְךָ."—xxiv. 19, "And if a man cause a blemish in his neighbour בַּעֲמִיתוֹ; as he hath done so shall be done to him."—xxv. 14, "And if thou sell ought unto thy neighbour לַעֲמִיתְךָ, or buyest ought of thy *neighbour's* hand, ye shall not oppress a man his brother. According to the number of years after the jubilee, thou shalt buy of thy neighbour עֲמִיתְךָ. Ye shall not, therefore, oppress a man his neighbour עֲמִיתוֹ; but thou shalt fear thy God," &c. These are the

* Hengstenberg Christologie, p. ii. p. 334.

only places where it occurs, and in all these it is synonymous with brother, or fellow. It expresses the relation of fellow-Israelite, or fellow-man, and points out an identity of nature, which is the very ground on which doing evil to our neighbour is forbidden. When, therefore, God calls any being עֲמִיתִי "My fellow," it necessarily implies that that being stands in the same relation to God as one Israelite or man does to another; that is, that he is of the same nature or substance, that is, that he is very God. It cannot be urged that there is no being, who can be considered as God's fellow, for Zechariah himself, in ch. ii. and iii., speaks of a being who is sent, and is, therefore, the angel of the Lord, and yet who is the Lord, and we have shown, in the observations on ch. i., that this is the general representation of the Old Testament Scriptures. Neither can it be said that this divine character is inconsistent with the other representations of Messiah. Malachi says, "The Lord הָאָדוֹן whom ye seek shall suddenly come to his temple," (Mal. iii. 1.), where the divine title אָדוֹן with the article הָ, which is never given to any being but God, is applied to the Messiah, as the Jewish commentators acknowledge. R. Alshech, in his Commentary on the passage, even goes so far as to assert that the coming of the Messiah includes in it the coming of God. He says, "It is well known that in the coming of the Messiah is [included] the coming of the blessed God into the world to fulfil the verse, 'Arise, shine, for thy light is come,' and again, 'I will dwell in the midst of thee.'"* And again, Jeremiah says, "This is his name whereby he shall be called, The Lord יהוה our Righteousness," (xxiii. 6), both of which names imply a participation of the divine attributes, as the same Rabbi well expounds in his Commentary on

* וידוע כי בביאת המשיח היא ביאתו יתברך אל העולם לקיים מקרא הכתוב קומי אורי כי בא אורך ואומר ושכנתי בתוכך ׃

Jeremiah: "Messiah is called the Lord our Righteousness, that is to say, through the superabundance of his righteousness and purity, righteousness will be communicated to Israel from heaven. Messiah will be like a reservoir into which it is poured, and from whence it is spread amongst all the people; and this is the meaning of 'The Lord our Righteousness.' That is to say, that as the LORD sends forth righteousness to him that comes to be cleansed, and still more to the clean, so also the Messiah shall be like the blessed God, and his name shall be called 'The Lord our Righteousness,' for from Thee our righteousness shall be derived as from the Lord."* Many other similar passages might be adduced, but these are sufficient to remove the objection that the description of divinity is foreign from Messiah's character. The sum of all that has been said is, that the words, "Awake, O sword, against my shepherd, and the man that is my fellow—Smite the Shepherd, and the sheep shall be scattered," are spoken of the Messiah—that, therefore, Messiah was to come before the scattering of the sheep, i. e., before the destruction of the temple; that he was to be smitten, and that then the Jews were to be dispersed. It is very easy to show that these particulars were fulfilled in Jesus of Nazareth. He came at the time here predicted, he was smitten, and very soon after the Jews were dispersed, and remain dispersed to this day.

The only objection that can be made is, that he was not slain by the sword, whereas Zechariah says, "Awake, O sword," but this is easily answered, as Hengstenberg has shown: "Sword" is employed figuratively to express violent death by the hands of others, as Nathan says to David, "Thou hast killed Uriah, the Hittite, with the

* ומשיח ה׳ צדקנו לומר ע״י שפע צדקו וכשרון יושפע לישראל מן השמים ויהי׳ המשיח כצנור שיורק בעצם בו וממנו יתפשט בכל העם וזהו ה׳ צדקנו לומר כאשר ה׳ משפיע צדקות לבא ליטהר ומה גם לטהור כך המשיח ידמה לו ית׳ ויקרא שמו ה׳ צדקנו כי ממך ימשך צדקנו כאשר מה׳ ;

sword," 2 Sam. xii. 9, whereas it appears, from xi. 24, that he had been shot with a missile weapon. A similar instance occurs in the words of the Israelites to Moses and Aaron, " Ye have made our savour to be abhorred in the eyes of Pharaoh, and in the eyes of his servants, to put a sword into their hands to slay us." (Exod. v. 21).

CHAPTER XIV.

1. "*Behold the day cometh to the Lord.*"—That day shall be to the Lord, for his glory and his might shall be seen at that time, and that is the time when Gog and Magog shall come against the land of Israel, as the Prophet Ezekiel has prophesied.

"*And thy spoil shall be divided in the midst of thee.*"—This is spoken of Jerusalem, for the heathen shall divide the spoil of the city in the midst of it, as it is said, "The houses shall be rifled." But Jonathan has interpreted, "Behold, the day that shall come from before the Lord, and the house of Israel shall divide the wealth of the nations in the midst of thee, Jerusalem."

2. "*For I will gather;*" that is to say, he will put it into their heart to come to Jerusalem to war, as it is said in the prophecy of Ezekiel, "And I will cause thee to come up from the north parts, and will bring thee upon the mountains of Israel" (xxxix. 2.).

"*And the city shall be taken.*"—This affliction shall be for the purifying of the third which shall be left in it; and in reference to this, it is said in the prophecy of Isaiah, "Hide thyself, as it were, for a little moment, until the indignation be overpast" (xxvi. 20.). And it is said, in the prophecy of Daniel, "There shall be a time of trouble, such as never was since there was a nation," &c. (xii. 1.).

And the houses rifled."—נָשַׁסּוּ one of the reduplicating verbs, the root is שָׁסַס, and so we find in מִי נָתַן לִמְשִׁסָּה יַעֲקֹב "who gave Jacob for a spoil" (Isaiah xlii. 24), the meaning is plundering or spoiling.

"*And half of the city shall go forth into captivity;*

i. e., They shall lead them from the city forth as captives to their tents, which are outside the city. Thus far the blessed God will leave them in the power of their enemies to purify them, and every one that is written in the book shall be delivered, and shall receive the affliction cheerfully.

"*And the residue of the people shall not be cut off from the city.*"—For God will not give them again into the hand of their enemies, but Israel shall prevail against their enemies, by the help of God, who is with them, and this is what is said, "The Lord shall go forth."

3. "*Then the Lord shall go forth —— as* בְּיוֹם קְרָב, *in the day of battle.*" The Chaldee for מלחמה is קרבא. And so we read טוֹבָה חָכְמָה מִכְּלֵי קְרָב, "Wisdom is better than weapons of war" (Eccles. ix. 18), and there are other like instances. Here it is said, "in the day of battle;" but what battle is not explained. The meaning is according to the Targum, "As the day when he waged war at the Red Sea," for then Israel was in great affliction, for the Egyptians were pursuing after them, and Moses, our master, peace be upon him, said, "The Lord shall fight for you, and ye shall hold your peace" (Exod. xiv. 14.). And so it is said, "And fight against those nations."

4. "*And his feet shall stand.*"—This is said figuratively, because a sign and wonder shall be exhibited in the Mount of Olives, in its cleaving asunder. And that great wise man, our master, Moses, may his memory be blessed, has interpreted "his cause" as ויברך אתך לרגלי, "and the Lord hath blessed thee at my foot" (Gen. xxx. 30), i. e., on my account. In the same way [he would take] רַגְלָיו, i. e., "His causes shall stand, that is to say, the miracles which shall then be seen in that place, of which God is the cause, i. e. the author."* And Jonathan has interpreted, "And he shall be revealed in his might at that time."

* See Moreh Nevuchim, part i. cap. xxviii.

"*The Mount of Olives, which is before Jerusalem.*"—i. e. near Jerusalem, on the east of it.

"*In the midst thereof, toward the east and toward the west.*"—From the east to the west the whole mountain shall be split, half of it to the north, and half of it to the south, and there shall be between them a very great valley. וּמָשׁ signifies shall be removed; that is to say, one half of the mountain shall be moved out of its place to the north side, and the other half to the south, and the valley between. So Jonathan has interpreted וּמָשׁ, "shall remove," by ויתלש, "shall be torn up." And this sign is a type of the cleaving of the Gentiles who come against Jerusalem, and who shall fall scattered about.

5. "*And ye shall flee to the valley of the mountains.*"—When the mountain is split, they shall flee from before the voice of the earthquake, and they shall flee to the valley of the mountains.

"*For the valley of the mountains shall reach to Azal.*"—For the valley which shall be made by this cleft shall extend and reach to Azal, which is the name of a place. That is to say, outside the mountains this cleft shall extend to Azal, and they shall flee thither, thinking to be delivered outside the mountains; but they shall find the valley there as elsewhere. הָרַי is the same as הָרִים. There are other examples of this form, as אַצִּילֵי יָדַי (armholes, Ezek. xiii. 18,) for יָדַיִם. And again, וְקָרַע לוֹ חַלּוֹנָי, "And cutteth him out windows" (Jer. xxii. 14), for חַלּוֹנִים. And again, חֲשׂוּפַי שֵׁת, the same as חֲשׂוּפִים (Isaiah xx. 4). And there are other similar instances, as we have written in the book Michlal.

"*Like as ye fled.*"—That is to say, as your fathers fled, and so it is said, "*And he brought us out from thence*" (Deut. vi. 23), and other similar passages.

"*Before the earthquake.*"—Some say that this is what is said in Isaiah, "And the posts of the door moved," that the earthquake took place at that time. And that is what is said at the beginning of Amos, "Two years before the earthquake" (Amos i. 1.).

"*And the Lord my God shall come.*"—וּבָא signifies אָז יָבֹא, then he shall come, as it is said, "The Lord shall go forth." "All the saints," is to be interpreted as if there were a conjunction, "*And* all the saints." Similar cases are שֶׁמֶשׁ יָרֵחַ, "The sun *and* moon" (Hab. iii. 11); רְאוּבֵן שִׁמְעוֹן, Reuben *and* Simeon (Exod. i. 2); מֶלֶךְ שָׂרִים, "King and princes" (Hos. viii. 10), &c. "Saints" means angels, as it is said, "He shall give his angels charge over thee" (Ps. xci. 11); and "thither cause thy mighty ones to come down, O Lord" (Joel iii. 11.). עִמָּךְ, "with thee," refers to Jerusalem, just as "in the midst of thee" does in the first verse. Jonathan has interpreted עמך by עמיה, "with him;" and that great wise man, Rambam,* of blessed memory, has interpreted this of the good promise which he promised Israel by the hands of his holy prophets. And he has interpreted "The Lord my God shall come," by means of all the saints with thee who spake to Israel.

Jonathan has interpreted וְנַסְתֶּם, at the beginning of the verse, by וְיִסְתְּתִים, "It shall be shut;" as if he read וְנִסְתַּם similar to נִכְתָּם עֲוֹנֵךְ, "Thine iniquity is marked" (Jer. ii. 22), and so it is found in some copies; and it is said that the men of the East read thus ונסתם. If this be the reading, the meaning will be, that after the cleaving open of the Mount of Olives, it will be shut again, an hour or hours, a day or days after, and thus the miracle will be so much the greater, that it should be shut after splitting open; for in the common earthquakes, by which the earth is split open, it does not close again. Such was the opening of the earth which happened to Korah and his company, for the earth closed after it had been split open, as it is said, "And the earth covered them," and this was a great miracle. The meaning of

* Moreh Nevuchim, part i. 22.

the words, "The valley of the mountains shall reach unto Azal," will then be, that as to the valley which was made between the two halves of the mountain, when it is closed up, its closure shall reach to the highest place in the mountain, so that it cannot be said that it is half, or two parts, closed, but that it is entirely closed, even to the highest spot in the mountain. אָצַל means something high, as וְאֶל אֲצִילֵי בְּנֵי יִשְׂרָאֵל, "and upon the nobles of the children of Israel" (Exod. xxiv. 11), where אצילי means the great ones of Israel. As to the expression, "mountains," though the Mount of Olives is only one mountain, yet when split it becomes two.

6. "*And it shall come to pass in that day.*"—In that day in which he says that this miracle shall occur, there shall also be this circumstance, that the light shall neither be יְקָרוֹת, "precious," nor קִפָּאוֹן, "thickness." The meaning is figurative, that the light of that day shall not be bright, which is the meaning of אוֹר יְקָרוֹת, as וְיָרֵחַ יָקָר הוֹלֵךְ, "or the moon walking in brightness" (Job xxxi. 26), nor light of thickness, i. e. dense and thick, which is like darkness. The sense is, the day shall not be entirely light nor entirely dark, i. e. it shall not pass entirely in tranquillity nor in affliction, for they two shall be in it, and so he says afterwards, not day and not night. Jonathan has interpreted, "There shall be nothing that day, but privation and coagulation" [Scil. of the light.].

7. "*But it shall be one day.*"—That day shall be a day set apart to the Lord, in which he shall be known by his mighty deeds and his wonders, which he shall then do.

"*Not day nor night.*"—Not entirely day, nor entirely night; that is to say, it shall not be all affliction, nor all tranquillity.

"*But at evening time it shall be light.*"—At the time when the affliction is the greatest, when the city goes forth into captivity, then the Lord shall go forth and fight with those nations.

8. "*And it shall be that living waters.*"—This is what is said in the prophecy of Joel, "A fountain shall come forth from the house of the Lord" (Joel iii. 18); and, as is said in the prophecy of Ezekiel, "And behold, there ran out waters" (Ezek. xlvii. 2.). And it is said there, that they became a great river, as is written in that chapter.

"*The former* sea."—The eastern.

"*The hinder* sea."—The western. That is what is said in the prophecy of Ezekiel, "And go into the sea" (Ezek. xlvii. 8.)

"*In summer and in winter shall it be;*"—i. e., Their going forth, for these streams shall not dry up, and their waters shall not fail. And Jonathan has interpreted, "In summer and in winter they shall go forth." The wise man, R. Abraham Aben Ezra Zal has written, that summer and winter are mentioned because they are the dry seasons, for the days of summer are hot and dry, and the days of winter are cold and dry, and at these times the rivers fail.

9. "*And the Lord shall be King.*"—When the Gentiles, who come against Jerusalem, see these wonders that are mentioned, they will acknowledge that the Lord reigns over all the earth, and disposes all sublunary things, and does therein according to his will, and reverses the course of nature to do the will of those that fear him: for all things are the work of his hands.

"*In that day there shall be one Lord, and his name one.*"—For they shall acknowledge that the Lord is one, and there is no God beside him, and thus his name shall be one, for in the whole world they shall not mention the name of another God, but shall mention his name only, as it is written above, "It shall come to pass in that day, saith the Lord of Hosts, that I will cut off the names of the idols out of the land, and they shall no more be remembered" (xiii. 2). But the wise man, R. Abraham Aben Ezra Zal, has explained this of the Shem-hammephorash, which is the four-lettered * name, and he has written thus:—"His name one, this is the glorious name made known to us through Moses our master, peace be upon him, and it shall be pronounced then by the mouth of all, as it is written." The great wise man, the Rav, † Rabbi Moses, has also explained it of the Shem-hammephorash, for all the names given to God are derivative names, taken either from the nature of his works, or as an intimation of his perfection; and as these derivative names are many, some of the children of men have thought that the blessed God has as many attributes as the number of the works from which the names are derived; and therefore he has promised to communicate to the children of men so much understanding as will remove this doubt, and says, "In that day there shall be one Lord, and his name one;" that is to say, that as he is one, so he shall then be called by only one name, and that shall point out his substance, and shall not be derivative. Jonathan has also interpreted, "The kingdom of the Lord shall be revealed."

10. "*All the land shall be compassed as a plain.*"—All the land which is round about Jerusalem, which is now mountains, as it is said, "The mountains are round about Jerusalem" (Ps. cxxv. 2), shall then be level as a plain, but it itself shall be exalted, and high above all the earth. Although it is at present higher than all the land of Israel, yet on account of the mountains which are round about it, its height does not appear; but in that time, when all the country round about it is a plain, its height above all the land will be visible; as it is said in the prophecies of Isaiah, "The mountain of the Lord's house shall be established in the top of the mountains, and shall be exalted above the hills." And although the meaning there is, exalted in greatness and dignity, it shall be fulfilled in both senses.

* Literally, son of four letters.

† Moreh Nevuchim, part. i. c. 61.

"*From Gebah to Rimmon.*"—From thence the plain shall commence נֶגֶב יְרוּשָׁלָם, south of Jerusalem.

וְרָאֲמָה, "It shall be lifted up," with an Aleph mobile, instead of the ו, the second radical, like the Aleph in וְקָאם שָׁאוֹן, "a tumult shall arise" (Hos. x. 14), except that the Aleph here is quiescent. The meaning of וְרָאֲמָה is, as we have written, that it shall be exalted, and high above all the earth.

"*And inhabited in her place.*"— תַחְתֶּיהָ, She shall be in her place, only that she shall be lengthened and widened.

שַׁעַר הַפִּנִּים.—This is what is called in Jeremiah שַׁעַר הַפִּנָּה, "the gate of the corner," and there the tower of Hananeel is also mentioned (Jer. xxxi. 38.).

"*The king's wine-presses.*"—The threshing-floor and the wine-press, and it was known to them that they were near the outside of the city. Jonathan has interpreted "To the king's pits."

11. "*And men shall dwell in it.*"—The meaning is, They shall dwell in it for ever.

"*And there shall be no more utter destruction.*"—It shall not become an anathema and desolation for ever, according as it is said in the prophecy of Jeremiah, "It shall not be plucked up, nor thrown down any more for ever" (Jer. xxxi. 40.).

12. "*And this shall be the plague wherewith the Lord will smite —— Their flesh consume away.*" — This is the falling off of the limbs.

"*While they stand upon their feet.*"—That it should not happen after sickness, but whilst still standing upon his feet, his flesh and limbs should melt away.

"*In their holes.*"—When their eyes consume away, their place will be a hole. Jonathan has interpreted "Their eyes shall melt away in their orbs." This plague is that which is said in the prophecy of Isaiah, "And I will set a sign amongst them, and I will send those that escape" (Isaiah lxvi. 19.).

13. "*And his hand shall rise up against the hand of his neighbour.*"—עלתה [means] his hand shall consume away, when he lays hold of the hand of his neighbour, as it is said, "Their flesh shall consume away." עָלָה is taken in this sense in כַּעֲלוֹת גָּדִישׁ בְּעִתּוֹ, "like as a shock of corn cometh in in his season" (Job v. 26.). And again, וַתַּעַל שִׁכְבַת הַטָּל, when the lying of the dew ceased" (Exod. xvi. 14.); and again, וְעָרֶיהָ עָלָה, "Her cities have ceased"* (Jer. xlviii. 15); and so Jonathan has interpreted, "His hand shall be torn off with the hand of his fellow."

14. "*And Judah also.*"—The meaning is, Judah also, who came along with the Gentiles, and made war with them at Jerusalem, when they shall see the plague which the Lord will send amongst them, they shall gather their wealth, gold and silver, and apparel; as it is said, "They shall devour on the right hand and on the left." The expression וְאֻסַּף, "shall be gathered," means it shall be gathered by their hands first, and afterwards the inhabitants of Jerusalem shall go forth, and they shall also plunder. Jonathan has interpreted, "They also of the house of Judah," &c.

16. "*And it shall come to pass, every one that is left.*" —Those that are left are they who have laid it to heart during the battle, and have turned to the Lord with all their heart.

"*The King the Lord of Hosts.*"—For they have acknowledged him as king over all the earth.

"*The feast of tabernacles.*"—According as the war has been at that time, and they have seen the wonders of the Creator, blessed be He, so they shall come from year to year to the remembrance of that day.

17. "*And it shall be——upon them shall be no rain.*" —Upon the land whose inhabitants will not go up, no rain shall descend in that year.

18. *And if the family of Egypt——that have no rain.*"

* So Kimchi explains these words.

—But upon them no rain descends any year, and they have no need of rain. If so, what will be their punishment? (Answer.) There shall be the plague wherewith the Lord shall smite all the heathen who come up against Jerusalem, as it is said, "Their flesh shall consume away.

"*That come not up to keep the feast of tabernacles.*" —Because the children of Egypt come not up to keep the feast of tabernacles, they shall have this punishment, that the plague shall be upon them. Jonathan has interpreted, "The Nile shall not rise for them, but there shall be upon them the plague wherewith the Lord will smite," &c.

19. "*This shall be the sin of Egypt, and the sin of all nations.*"—The sin of Egypt is the plague, and the sin of all the nations is, that the rain shall not descend, as has been mentioned.

חַטַּאת [sin] means punishment, that is to say, the punishment of sin; and in this way it is said, "The iniquity of the Amorite is not yet full;" that is to say, the punishment of the iniquity. Jonathan has interpreted it by פורענות.

20. "*In that day there shall be upon the bells of the horses, Holiness to the Lord.*"— מְצִלּוֹת are those that hang on the necks of the horses, and they are scales. These bells shall be holiness to the Lord, for they shall make of them pots wherein to boil in the house of the sanctuary. And as to these horses, some interpret that they are the horses which shall die in the plague, as has been said. And others interpret that they are the horses of those who go up from year to year to keep the feast of tabernacles, who will devote the bells of their horses in order to make pots of them, wherein to boil in the temple. And the meaning of "upon the bells," is, it shall be, as it were, written and engraved upon them, "Holiness to the Lord," so they shall be known that they are holiness, and no man will take of them for himself, not even one. And in the words of our rabbies, of blessed memory, it is said, "What is the meaning of upon the מְצִלּוֹת of the horses?"

R. Joshua, the son of Levi, says, the Holy One, blessed be He, will enlarge Jerusalem, until the hour when the horse runs and makes a shadow. (The meaning is, until midday, for then the horse makes a shadow underneath himself.) * R. Eliezer says, the bells which hang between the horses' eyes shall be holiness to the Lord.

"*The pots in the Lord's house shall be like the bowls.*"—The meaning is, as many as the bowls, and so Jonathan has interpreted, "Many as the bowls," according as the bowls in the house of the Lord, for sprinkling the blood, shall be many, for the sacrificers shall be many. For all who come up to keep the feast of tabernacles shall bring sacrifices.

21. "*Yea, every pot.*"—They shall increase the pots, on account of the multitude of the sacrifices; for they shall not have sufficient in those which are in the house of the Lord; but every pot in Jerusalem and Judah shall be holiness to the Lord, therein to boil the sacrifices of the peace-offerings. And when the Gentile sacrificers shall come, they shall take of them, and cook in them.

"*There shall be no more the Canaanite.*"—Jonathan has interpreted this, "There shall be no more he that maketh merchandise;" as "her merchants, כנעניה, are the honourable of the earth;" that is to say, her סוחריה. That is to say, the house of the Lord shall no longer need a merchant to sell pots there, or brass whereof to make pots; for the voluntary devoters of property will be many. But my lord my father says, that this refers to the Gibeonites, for it is said of them that they were hewers of wood and drawers of water in the temple; but they shall not be there any more, for the great ones of the Gentiles shall serve the priests, and this is the meaning of the words, "I will take of them for priests and Levites."

* Pesachim, fol. 50, 1. See also Wagenseil. Tela Ig. on the last page of vol. i.

ERRATA.

Page 3, line 24, insert a dagesh in the ל.
— 8, — 23, for ווקה, read קָוֶה.
— 9, — 15, for מָלְאָךְ, read מַלְאָךְ.
— 55, — 18, for יְרוּשָׁלַם, read יְרוּשָׁלַםִ.
— ib., — 20, for שָׁאוּל, twice, read שָׁאוֹל.
— 56, — 34, for לָקוֹח, read לָקוֹחַ.
— 64, last line but two, for מִתַּהְתָּיו, read מִתַּחְתָּיו.
— 70, last line but seven, for וַיֵּרֵד read וַיֵּרֶד.
— 77, line 27, for שַׂדָה, read הַשָּׂדֶה.

www.ingramcontent.com/pod-product-compliance
Lightning Source LLC
La Vergne TN
LVHW050636100826
845148LV00011B/1880

* 9 7 8 1 5 5 6 3 5 3 2 9 1 *